STIRLING V
The Story of the SAS in WWII

STEVE STONE

© Steve Stone 2014

Steve Stone has asserted his rights under the Copyright, Design and Patents Act, 1988, to be identified as the author of this work. All rights reserved. No part of this publication may be reproduced in any form or by any means electrical, mechanical, including photocopying, recording or any information storage without permission in writing from the author.

Published by Digital Dream Publishing 2014

Introduction

What the SAS (Special Air Service) did during World War Two was to revolutionise the way wars could be fought, and in many ways, became the blueprint that would be later used by Special Forces across the globe. Delta Force in the late 1960s based themselves on the SAS and their doctrine. What was learnt in those early years of the SAS, proved invaluable for setting up techniques and tactics that are still relevant today. The SAS were true pioneers and made a small yet significant impact during the war. David Stirling's thoughts was to throw out standard military tactics – the SAS was trained to use improvisation rather than follow set military doctrine. This improvisation and adjusting of tactics depending on the objective was at the heart of the SAS successes during the war. They would make do with the kit they had, even borrow or steal kit, even from the enemy to accomplish a mission or objective. This is where the true motto of "Who Dares Wins" can trace its roots back to.

Even after David Stirling was captured as a prisoner of war, the SAS continued to grow under new leadership, adapting and growing. Until being disbanded after the end of World War II. Only to reconstitute as 21 SAS a Territorial Army unit before becoming a regular unit in the form of 22 SAS based at Hereford. Without David Stirling and the SAS, we would never have had Bravo Two Zero, Libyan Embassy hostage rescue and countless other SAS operations. All these men are trained to be the best of the best, suffer unimaginable hardship, operating deep behind enemy lines. Whilst the enemy, maybe different, the tactics and types of missions, are not too dissimilar to the ones undertaken by the SAS in World War II. High technology is still no replacement for boots on the ground, which can react and gather intelligence, in ways that technology still cannot. Highly trained soldiers such as the SAS can help reduce the need for larger scale war and military deployment, by their ability to be used as a surgical tool.

The SAS 'Originals' in the early days had an uphill battle to impress those higher up in command. Even then, at times, military planners did not understand how the SAS could be better utilised, which was a major frustration to the regimental commanders. It was the unconventional warfare that David Stirling had undertaken in 8 Commando that began to lead him to formulate a plan of a more specialized force. At the same time, Jock Lewes had similar thoughts to Stirling before joining Stirling in his venture. They both believed that a small group of like-minded, highly trained and dedicated men could cause havoc to the Germans. Stirling's approach was to think of war in three dimensions. Stirling looked at warfare sideways and almost an amateur perspective. He saw killing the enemy as just one aspect. By using surprise and guile you could also disorientate, alarm, and embarrass the enemy then the impact of the raid would be intensified.

Early in training with the commando's including Jock Lewes, Stirling was injured in a parachute jump. As he jumped out of an aircraft, his parachute became caught on the tail fin and ripped a hole in his parachute taking out a couple of panels. Stirling plummeted to the ground at twice the speed he should have done due to the torn panels. The force of the impact caused severe spinal damage and Stirling lost consciousness. It would be eight weeks before he got any feeling back in his legs and longer still before he could walk properly. The accident would leave Stirling with back pain and migraines for the rest of his life. In total, Stirling spent two months in hospital much to Stirling's frustration. This time spent recovering was not wasted on Stirling and helped to secure the SAS's future. He dedicated his time to the actual planning, something he had been unable to do whilst undertaking intense training. He put in place his exact requirements for the regiment from its purpose to the selection and training of the men. Using unorthodox methods that are now associated with the SAS - Stirling took his plan straight to the top. Rather than going through the normal chain of command, where the potential for the SAS was instantly seen. Stirling realised that if he went through the chain of command, it would be 'binned' by the more cautious and in his words "fossilised shit" of the staff officers.

After sneaking into the Middle East Headquarters by using his crutches to climb over the perimeter wire and then being pursued by two guards. Stirling found General Sir Neil Ritchie, taking him by surprise, Stirling handed him a condensed version of his proposal, which Ritchie found interesting. Ritchie, forgetting how Stirling had come to appear in his office such was his interest in Stirling's proposal. A few days later, this led to a meeting with General Sir Claude Auchinleck who was a family friend of the Stirling's. Along with Ritchie and Major General Eric Dorman-Smith. All three saw the potential in Stirling's proposal and how it could aid in reversing the tide against Rommel.

This led to the birth of a regiment that has now become world renowned. It has not been without sacrifice, though, with SAS soldiers killed in action during World War II and in subsequent conflicts and wars.

This book covers the key operations from the first ill-fated SAS operation in Libya to the final missions at the end of the war in Germany, including the discovery of the horrific Belson concentration camp. It is an impressive story where David Stirling may have been the instigator, but his dedicated officers and men also played an important part in moulding and developing the SAS. Stirling even recognised the fact he had 'five co-founders.' Much of what was learned in those early years is still being used 60 years later. This book is dedicated to all those that fell during the Second World War, trying to bring peace and security back from a world in turmoil and another horrific world war.

Chapter One

North Africa, 1941

Rommel had the upper hand, but, according to Stirling, he had left himself vulnerable; his lines of communication and airfields along the coast were crying out to be attacked. Erwin Rommel, also known as, the 'Desert Fox' was in command of the Afrika Korps, which was the German expeditionary force in Libya and Tunisia during the North African Campaign of World War Two. The North African Campaign had begun on the 10 June 1940. The campaign was fought between the Allies and Axis powers, many of whom had interests in Africa dating back from the late 19th century. The Allied war effort was dominated by the British Commonwealth along with exiles from German-occupied Europe. American forces joined in the campaign after entering the war on December 8, 1941, the day after Peral Harbour. They began direct military assistance in North Africa on 11 May 1942.

Fighting in North Africa started with the Italian's declaration of war on 10 June 1940. On 14 June, the British Army's 11th Hussars and assisted by elements of the 1st Royal Tank Regiment, crossed the border from Egypt into Libya and captured the Italian Fort Capuzzo. This was followed by an Italian counteroffensive into Egypt and the capture of Sidi Barrani in September 1940 and then in December 1940 by a Commonwealth counteroffensive, Operation Compass. During Operation Compass, the Italian 10th Army was destroyed, and the German Afrika Korp were dispatched to North Africa to reinforce Italian forces to prevent a complete Axis defeat. A series of battles for control of Libya and parts of Egypt followed, with one side and then the other gaining the upper hand. The campaign reached its climax with the Second Battle of El Alamein and the Axis final defeat.

It was during Stirling's time as a commando in North Africa, that Stirling identified that commando units had failed simply due to being too large. A smaller team, with the element of surprise and using guerrilla warfare, would do a far better job. In his usual, almost arrogant manner, Stirling said what they needed, was a small, handpicked team of men, that were well trained and could parachute into the desert behind enemy lines and attack thirty targets in a one night raid. He took this idea as a young officer straight to General Ritchie, who saw it as the sort of plan that may work and was prepared to discuss it with the commander in chief. Three days later, Stirling was ordered back, promoted to Captain and given the green light to form the first SAS team with six officers and 60 NCOs (Non-Commissioned Officers) and warrant officers. It was on the orders of Brigadier Dudley Clark that the unit would be called 'L' Detachment, Special Air Service Brigade. Clark was involved in counterintelligence and counter espionage. He saw the actual missions the SAS would undertake as a way of reinforcing his idea. Clark had already planted fake photographs in Egyptian newspapers. Even having two men wander around Egypt in fake uniforms pretending to be SAS paratroopers. Clarke was arrested in October 1941 in Madrid by the Spanish Police as an elegantly dressed women. This was all part of Clark' funny, charming and slightly odd character.

Clark's idea behind the First Special Air Service Brigade was to unsettle Rommel by making him think the British had a new and upcoming airborne brigade, Stirling later thought the 'L' stood for learner. Stirling set about recruiting; the first to be recruited was a man called John (Jock) Lewes, a rather humourless character with great focus and no time for frivolity. In many respects, he was almost the opposite of Stirling. Stirling and Lewes had been in the commandos together. Lewes was unsure if Stirling and took quite a bit of persuasion to get him on board.

Lewes was born in Calcutta and grew up in Australia before joining the Welsh Guard, he co-founded the SAS with Stirling. Lewes brought with him Guardsmen Davis, Almonds, an American Riely, Blakeney, a former trawler man, and Lilley. Stirling did the rounds of various commando units, trying to tempt soldiers into joining him. With many sitting around in the desert feeling bored, it did not take much persuasion from Stirling with the lure of action. As well as the NCOs, Stirling still required another five officers; these were in the form of

Thomas, Bonnington and McGonigal, a southern Irishman who recommended a fellow Irishman, Mayne. Paddy Mayne had joined the Royal artillery in the Supplementary Reserve severing with several units until he joined the 11 Command. The final officer to be recruited was Fraser.

Stirling went around picking up commandos sitting around in the desert doing not much at all at the time. They were unconventional 'rouges' the usual soldier type. Stirling interviewed everyone who volunteered, asking some quite probing questions, before declaring who he did and did not want. His questions were direct, and he had no time for any waffle. Stirling was a very charismatic individual and, at 6'6", a very tall individual, too. He was the son of a brigadier general, was educated at Ampleforth College. His heart always yearned for action and adventure; he was due to climb Mount Everest when war broke out in 1939. He ended up in the Scots Guards Supplemental Reserves before joining 8 Commando. He gained his men's respect almost instantaneously; many of those men had no time for officers in the first place.

Once recruited, these new SAS recruits were all sent out to Kabrit in Egypt, which was roughly 90 miles east of Cairo, right on the edge of the Great Bitter Lake. It had none of the niceties of Cario; they were greeted by fly-ridden tents and plenty of sand and dust. During World War II, the facility was known as RAF Station Kabrit, (Landing Ground 213) and was a major Royal Air Force facility which was used during the Western Desert Campaign. The desert was sometimes flat sometimes undulating with exposed rocks and plenty of sand. It was sometimes broken by the odd bit of scrub or desert grass. Any exposed rocks were bleached by the sun. With temperatures ranging from 120 degrees during the day and below freezing at night, it was a hostile environment with death ever present.

With supplies, low, a few of the men went along to do what, in Army slang, is called 'tactical relocation'. Put simply, they stole a truck, some three- and four-man tents, chairs, tables, pots and pans and even a piano. The New Zealand soldiers who normally occupied the area were away on exercise. In many ways, you could say that was the very first SAS raid! Other provisions were sought by driving the truck to various camps dotted along the Suez Canal Zone. Whilst one of the lads, Kaufman distracted the quartermaster in conversation, Seekings and a couple of others loaded the truck up with anything useful. This turned the SAS training base into one of the best equipped in the area.

The training in those early months was relentless and hard, and with hard training comes a large appetite as the men soon burnt off calories. The search for supplies and equipment was left to Stirling, who travelled into Cairo on many occasions, fighting his unit's corner. Known also in Army slang as a 'bun fight' - something that still happens in many units to this day.

Lewes would constantly throw out challenges for the men to meet and then, when the men had met that challenge, he would throw out another, on the odd occasion demonstrating that if he could do it, so could the rest of his men. On the 16 October 1941, many of the men were down for their first parachute jump, along with several others. The Army had been experimenting with parachutes for about a year and everyone had undertaken some basic training, jumping off some wooden benches and even a moving truck to get them ready for their first jump. Stirling's SAS men sat in the back of the airplane, being buffeted around, and many of the men were quite pale through fear and airsickness. Some were shaking with nerves, and when they stood up their knees began to judder. The final shuffle to the door for many was the worst part, and it took a great deal of nerve for some of them to jump out. On jumping out, they tumbled for what seemed like an hour in their minds, but was in reality a few seconds, before seeing a white parachute burst open above and pull them the right way up. The landing was hard, but most were fine, with the odd bruise and twisted ankle here and there; later, Stirling lost his first man, Warburton; his chute failed to open, and he plummeted to the ground, hitting it with a very eerie thud.

Everyone knew at once he was dead. This was soon followed by Duffy, whose body landed quite close to Warburton. This hit the morale of 'L' Detachment quite hard. They had lost two great men before they had even gone into battle. A simple fitting on the static line had caused both deaths. As both the men had jumped, the pressure from the slipstream had buckled a clip, forcing the static line to disengage. This meant that their parachutes were not pulled open as they exited. This could have spelled the end for the SAS, but Stirling pushed them on, and they continued to train awaiting their first operation. As the harsh training continued there were dropouts, injuries and death. "Never run away. Because once you start running, you've stopped thinking." Decreed Lewes. He knew the best way to motivate men was to install the fear of failure, their fear of being 'returned to unit.' No one wanted to fail in front of their peers. One story gives an account of a soldier marching forty miles in just his socks as his boots gave way. The training built up strong bonds and an element of friction. The ones who remained knew they were part of an elite unit.

Stirling decide to demonstrate his units newly founded skills by undertaking a raid on the RAF 216 Bomber and Transport Squadron at Heliopolis airfield. The airfield was 94 miles away from Kabrit and Stirling had a £10 wager with the Group Captain that his men could creep in undetected. After the Group Captain stated it was an almost impossible feat.

On a moonless night, the SAS divided into five groups of ten set out. They marched at night and lay out under the hot sun during the day. On such small water rations, many hallucinating due to dehydration. On the fourth night, they reached the airfield. Cut their way through the barbed wire perimeter fence and stuck self-adhesive labels on the aircraft. Before silently leaving the airfield and making, their way to Army barracks in Abassea. They all looked in such a state the guards assumed they were surrendering Italian soldiers.

CHAPTER TWO

General Auchinleck's November 1941 offensive had been given the codename 'Crusader' and had two main elements to it. The first was to retake Cyrenaica in Libya and the second was to secure Libyan airfields that were currently in the hands of the Axis. If these objectives were achieved, supplies to Malta could be increased. The knock-on effect would be the ability to perform air raids on Sicily using the Libyan airfields. At the same time, Rommel was planning his own offensive, unbeknown to the Allies. Rommel's plan was also influenced by Malta. He knew that the further east he could push the British, the more the amount of air support the RAF could give to Malta would be diminished. It would also mean that German convoys sailing towards Malta would be able to get through more easily, and Rommel's hope was that this would ultimately lead to the defeat of the Allies in North Africa.

The British assault was due to start on 18 November 1941 and Rommel's new offensive was due to start a couple of days later. The Italians had tipped him off that they believed the British were on the verge of a new offensive; however, the Germans dismissed this. For 'L' Detachment, it was a small yet significant role that they were to play. On 16 November 1941, they were to parachute into the Libyan Desert before marching towards the coast and launching five separate raids on airfields between Gazzala and Tmimi. After this, they were to RV (Rendezvous) three miles southeast of Gadd-El-Ahmar at some crossroads, which were about 50 miles inland. At this point, they would be met by the LRDG (Long-Range Desert Group), which would then take them home.

The men learned about the operation called Operation Squatter on 15 November and it was the parachute jump that bothered most of the men more than anything. They all had to study the plans and ensure they knew the role they were to play in minute detail. The preparation of all kit, including explosives, was a very large task. At dawn on 16 November 1941, 54 SAS soldiers, along with Stirling, mounted aircraft and took off for their forward point of operations at Bagoush, 300 miles west of Kabrit. On arrival after a five-hour flight, the Stirling and his men found it amazing to see the lengths to which the RAF had gone to make them feel comfortable. The SAS had full use of the mess, including books, games and the wireless to entertain them. Each SAS man was given a bottle of beer as well.

At 1830, the SAS climbed into a fleet of trucks to make their way to the aircraft, which would convey them to the drop zone. Inside the aircraft, a Bristol Type 130A Bombay, it was rather cramped and initially quite warm. They had five Bristol Bombays in total for this mission, each capable of carrying up to 24 troops. With their fixed undercarriages and high mounted wings, they looked more like something from the First World War than the Second. They lumbered down the runway and into the sky, feeling as if they only just had enough power from their twin engines to get off the ground. As soon as the Bombays were at their ceiling of 18,000 feet, the men could not help but shiver uncontrollably as they were tossed around in the pitch-black dark. The darkness was soon broken by German searchlights lighting the planes up, followed quickly by flak. The flak was so thick and heavy that you could have almost walked across the sky on it.

Their fire seemed to become more and more accurate; on another aircraft the men saw a bullet fly in, just missing the auxiliary fuel tank, before going straight out into the night's sky, leaving an entry and exit hole in the fuselage. It was now eight minutes to go until they would be over the drop zone and to many those eight minutes seemed the longest ever. The Bombays and its occupants were now being tossed around quite violently by the incoming flak, unsure if they would make it to the drop zone before being blown out of the sky.

One by one, the men in one Bombay stood up and shuffled along like lemmings to a cliff, following each other out into the cold, dark night. They jumped out into a very strong wind that almost took their breath away; the noise of the wind rushing past drowned out the noise of the aircraft engines as they dropped to the ground. The darkness initially made it quite disorientating as they felt as if they were upside down. It was not until the men saw some of the dark landscape below that they could re-orientate themselves properly. It was still so dark that they did not even know if they were near the ground until they hit it hard and many giving out a small yelp. Many of the men were bruised and battered, some hitting rocks and even a thorny bush upon landing. Seekings got drag through a thorny bush and had blood dripping off him. For the SAS, this was an ominous start to the mission.

After landing, the next issue was releasing the chute before being dragged along the desert floor by the fierce wind. It took over an hour for all of the men to be rounded up by Lewes; such was the wide area over which they had been scattered by the wind. One of the lads, Cheyne, had broken his back upon landing. Lewes left him with some water and a pistol and that was the last Lewes and the rest of the men ever saw of him. It was hard, but a necessary choice that no one really wanted to make. For all they knew, he may well be still in the desert, lying in the same position in which he had been left; his remains possibly still waiting to be found to this day. His name is on the Alamein Memorial in Egypt for all the Allied soldiers with an unknown grave.

At just after 0030 they headed north towards the airfield, led by Du Vivier. The first three hours passed by without incident. At the three-hour point, it began to rain; it has been just a light shower initially, but it dampened their spirits a little, as they marched across the desert. It was not long until the terrain began to seem different from how it was depicted on their maps. They had travelled just over 15 miles and, with daylight looming; they had no choice but to lay up in some camel shrub until dark before setting off again. They spent the day sleeping; the silence was only broken by a German spotter plane flying overhead at quite a low altitude, although the men had no reason to believe they had been spotted. Just after midday, things started to take a turn for the worst with a torrential downpour that turned into a hailstorm with thunder and lightning. Such was the volume of water falling that after half an hour, the SAS men were waist deep in a torrent of water.

Lewes gave the order to move up to higher ground. Wearing just shorts and overalls, they were soaked to the skin, feeling quite miserable and cold - although they did not have to worry about not having enough water. Equipment including their bombs was rendered useless by the water.

Navigation had been difficult enough the previous night; this storm had now made it even harder for them. They were later told that it was one of the worst storms in local memory. By nightfall, with the storm still raging, Lewes made the decision to abort and head to the RV, where the LRDG would be waiting to pick them up. With the severe conditions, they were only able to make very slow progress; Many falling over a number of times as they slipped in the sandy mud. The desert had become a lake; at times, they were wading through water up to their knees. They could only stop and rest on high ground, and sometimes they would walk for over an hour before finding some higher ground that was dry.

All the men struggled, including Lewes, who gave temporary command to Riley, a senior sergeant who was an ex-guardsman and police officer. He pushed them along with a mixture of shouting and politely cajoling them along. All the while worrying about his men's wellbeing. Pretty much all the men were all frozen stiff, drenched to the skin and very hungry. Riley's motivation and command were probably the only reasons they all made it back alive. He would get them to march for 40 minutes then rest for 20 minutes. Finally, at sunrise the next morning, the storm started to abate. The weak sunshine brought some much-needed warmth to all the men. Their luck finally changed when they spotted a rough track called the Trig el Abd. This track went from the Egyptian border to Cyrenaica and would be their saviour as they marched along it through the night and into the next day.

All the men had already eaten their rations, which consisted of cheese, hard biscuits, dates and raisins. They also had an emergency chocolate ration. Many feeling weak, they ploughed on. Food was the only thing on many of the men's minds and they kept thinking of all the lovely things they would like to eat. Finally, late in the afternoon, Lewes spotted a signpost that told them how far they were from Bir-el-gubi and El Mechili This enabled them to find where they were on their maps. Much to their surprise, they were not that far from the RV. This gave the men the lift they needed to keep them going for the final stretch. Six hours later, at 2200, they were finally picked up by the LRDG, which to the men on seeing them was like seeing an angel. The SAS men's first request was some food, which consisted of bully beef, biscuits and tea. Out of all the other groups, only 21 out of the 55 who had jumped made it back to the RV. Stirling and Sgt Bait were the only two to make it back from their patrol. The roll of honour of good men lost seemed endless and left the remaining SAS men feeling numb. McGonical had died after he had broken his neck hitting the ground. He was twenty years old, and his death hit Paddy Mayne hard. Mayne was never the same after McGonigal's death. McGonigal was the only person who could calm Mayne's hot-tempered nature. Jim Almonds concerned about the fate of his comrades:

"The lads are now 280 miles inside enemy territory, hiding in the sand and awaiting dark to start their reign of terror and destruction. After the massacre is over and the enemy planes blown up, there remains that terrible march back through the desert. No one who is sick, or wounded can possibly make it, and none can afford to help. I am not there. I sit back in the safety of the camp and wish I were. Reality beats fiction for sheer, cold, calculating courage. Some of the lads cannot be beaten. Films and books of adventure fall far short of the real thing. More will be heard of the SAS should this raid go through as planned. My mates are somewhere in enemy territory. Poor devils, they need all the luck possible."

One Bombay flown by Flt alt Charlie West of the RAF. As they crossed, the coast at 300 feet effective anti-aircraft fire managed to hit the port engine, instruments (with a small piece of shrapnel getting stuck in the compass) and fuel tanks. The mission had to be aborted and the men headed for home.

However, the damage compass was sending them in a circle. Running low on fuel, West managed to land safely in the desert in an amazing fete of flying in a he worst storm in the area for fifty years. As dawn, broke and the storm died down. They were still dangerously close to the coast and ripe for air attack. Low on fuel West and the SAS men took to the air once more hopping to ditch near Tobruk. As the Bombay got to 200 feet, an Italian Breda machine gun opened on them from below. Bullets burst through the fuselage. A Bf 109 joined in the attack. A round from the 109 killed the navigator in the Bombay. West took evasive action but was not of much use against the highly manoeuvrable 109.

West crash-landed the Bombay on a series of low Sandhills sliding over them in such a rough manner some of the men inside were thrown clear. When the plane came to a stop. West had suffered broken ribs, fractured skull and internal injuries. The SAS prepared to make a stand. However, the presence of Axis ground forces meant any stand was hopeless and they all surrendered. Becoming POWs – West a year later would escape from a train taking him from Italy to Germany.

CHAPTER THREE

By the end of November 1941, the Eighth Army had lost its early gains against Rommel, and operation Crusader had been obliterated by Rommel's counterthrust which had penetrated Egypt. General Auchinleck was still convinced that Rommel had stretched his supply lines to the limit and was trying his best to bluff the British into retreating. Without supplies, especially fuel, Rommel's offensive would grind to a halt.

After the disastrous first mission for 'L' Detachment, all the men wondered if that would be the end of 'L' Detachment, and everyone would all be RTU'd (returned to units). Stirling was still very much of the mindset that he would not give up and that they would not parachute in next time, but would instead work with the LRDG, as they knew what they were doing. Many men after the last mission had some trepidation about going on another, but the men believed in Stirling and what he said made sense. Stirling never stopped thinking or planning how he could improve a mission. As he navigated back from the last mission, he was constantly evaluating and working out the exact cause of the current failed one. He had discussed why the raid had failed with Lloyd-Owen, who knew the perils of parachuting and simply said something like, "Might it not be more practical and less dangerous if the LRDG drove us to our targets?" The idea was that the SAS could be dropped off with all their equipment near to the target, and then the LRDG would pick them up again a few hours later.

This idea stuck and it was not long before, what was left of 'L' Detachment was at Siwa Oasis, the LRDG's base. Stirling asked the CO (Commanding Officer) if his plan was acceptable to him, and he saw no reason for it not to be. His only comment was that it must not interfere with any of the reconnaissance patrols that his unit was undertaking in the Libyan Desert. Stirling still had to go back to Cairo and convince his superiors that 'L' Detachment was not a failure and was still a very viable asset. He explained the rationale for why the raid had failed, but it was merely a gesture and there seemed no reason for 'L' Detachment to continue.

A chance encounter with Brigadier John Marriott would be Stirling's saviour. Stirling wanted to know if he had a unit that might be willing to accommodate Stirling's men for a while. Marriott told Stirling that Jalo Oasis in Libya had just been captured from the Italians and would suit Stirling and his men very well.

The LRDG was a reconnaissance and raiding unit, even Rommel, admitted that the LRDG caused more damage than any other British unit of equal strength.

It was initially called the LRP (Long Range Patrol) it was founded in June 1940 in Egypt by Major Bagnold, acting under the direction of General Wavell. Bagnold was assisted by Captain Shaw and Captain Clayton. Initially, most of the men came from New Zealand, but they were soon supplemented with Rhodesian and British volunteers. This led to the creation of some sub-units and the unit's name was to be LRDG. The LRDG never had a strength of more than 350 men, all of whom were volunteers.

The LRDG was formed to carry out deep penetration, covert reconnaissance patrols and intelligence missions from behind enemy lines, although they sometimes engaged in combat operations. Because the LRDG were experts in desert navigation, they were sometimes assigned to guide other units, as well as guiding Stirling's they also guided secret agents across the desert. During the North African Desert Campaign between December 1940 and April 1943, the vehicles of the LRDG operated constantly behind the Axis lines, missing a total of only 15 days during the entire period. One of their most notable offensive actions was during Operation Caravan, during an attack on the town of Barce and its associated airfield, on the night of 13 September 1942. The LRDG travelled 1,155 miles to reach their objective. One part of the force attacked the airfield claiming 35 aircraft destroyed, the other attacked the barracks. The LDRG lost ten men, three trucks and a jeep. What was seen as their most vital role was the 'Road Watch', during which they clandestinely monitored traffic on the main road from Tripoli to

Benghazi, transmitting the intelligence to the British Army Headquarters.

On 21 December 1941, the shortest day of the year, Fraser and his patrol were crouched down amongst some rocks. With the early morning mist gone, they could see the Germans digging defences in the early morning sunshine. They were all more interested in Agedabia aerodrome, which was just a few miles beyond the Germans, they could see digging. They took a note of the positions of the various aircraft and planned their escape route back to the RV and awaiting LRDG. An awful lot was riding on this raid; if it were a failure, it would most likely spell the end for 'L' Detachment. The men had spent a month at Jalo Oasis, training hard and carrying out some less significant raids, which had been successful on a smaller scale. Mayne, with one patrol, had managed to destroy 24 aircraft, but Stirling and Lewes had come up empty on their missions. Stirling had been told to put on a bit of a show at Agedabia. Fraser and his patrol had left in the back of a LRDG truck on 19 December and after a day's travel, they were dropped 16 miles away from the objective.

With them was Tait, who had designed a cap badge for 'L' Detachment - a flaming sword of Excalibur with the now well-known motto, 'Who Dares Wins'. It was actually Stirling who came up with 'Who Dares Wins' after Tait's first suggestion, 'Strike and Destroy,' followed by 'Descend to Ascend'. The actual wing dagger, which is now the standard cap badge, has a more conflicting story, with one source citing that it came from Roy Farran in 1948 and others attributing it to a SHAFE communique in 1944.

The five men crouching down were all travelling light, with just a revolver and eight Lewes bombs. Only one Thompson machine gun was being carried, along with four spare magazines. The actual Lewes bombs were designed by Lewes himself. Lewes had spent hours in an open makeshift laboratory experimenting with gun Cotton, gelignite and ammonal. What Lewes designed was a simple affair made from a plastic explosive and thermite, which were then rolled together and placed in a motor oil can. It was used with a No 27 detonator that looked like a biro pen. It was a glass tube containing acid and was primed by breaking the glass to allow the acid to eat through a wire and release the striking pin. You could adjust the timing by using thicker or thinner wire. They were colour-coded according to the length of the fuses. In practice, these bombs were highly effective; the thermite would cause a flash, which would ignite any fuel in an aircraft's wing, often sending the whole aircraft up in flames.

As they crouched behind the rocks, a goat herder with his herd grew close, very reminiscent of what happened nearly fifty years later with Bravo Two Zero. Like with Bravo Two Zero, the shepherd was a boy and he had climbed right up to where Fraser and his patrol lay hidden. He looked straight at them, but Fraser felt he would not go and tell the Germans and he carried on his way. At 1830, the men finally made their way towards the airfield. It was now dark and on the way, they were caught in the headlights of a German vehicle. Knowing that if they went prone or started to run, they would look even more suspicious, they just carried on walking and the German vehicle passed them by without stopping. They finally arrived at the airfield's perimeter at 2130 and spent a further three hours getting onto the airfield, ensuring they avoided any sentries and trip wires. Once on the airfield, they split up and placed their bombs on all the planes. It was a case of sneaking around in the shadows and keeping a watchful eye on any movement. The runway was used as a temporary RV where they could move back and forth after planting each bomb. They even found a sandbagged building which was full of aerial bombs, so they stuck a Lewes bomb in there too. With all the bombs planted, Fraser and his patrol made their way to the RV. They were about half a mile away before the first of the explosions broke the silence with an almighty roar. This was followed by a further 39 explosions, including an almost deafening roar as the building containing all the aerial bombs went up. The force of the blast was so large that Fraser and his patrol felt the concussion pressure of it.

At 0500, they made it back to the RV and awaiting LRDG. It had been a completely successful mission. They had got in and out unnoticed with not one casualty and given the Germans something to think about. In the end, Fraser and his patrol destroyed some 37 aircraft, leaving only two undamaged, simply due to running out of explosives. Fraser and his men got back to Jalo Oasis on 23 December and went straight into a celebration and a Christmas party, in honour of the fledgling SAS's most successful raid to date.

Chapter Four

After the successful 21 December 1941 raid, Stirling decided to have a second attempt at raiding Sirte and Tamit in Libya. The next day along with Mayne, Lewes was going attack Nofilia airfield. Fraser was off to Arco dei Fileni also in Libya, which the British had labelled as 'Marble Arch' - it was easier to say and it poked fun at Mussolini, who had built quite an ugly-looking towering arch. Stirling and Mayne left on Christmas Eve for their raid and the rest on Christmas Day. Fraser was dropped some six miles away from the Marble Arch airfield on 27 December, while Lewes's patrol, was dropped off 18 miles away from Nofilia airfield. The SASs drop-off point was also their RV point for the LDRG to come and pick them up. The men began their march across the desert and towards the airfield. Initially, the raid had gone to plan. The men had been able to sneak in through the perimeter without being seen, Lewes planted the first bomb and then Almonds planted the second. They then found the third plane, which they had not expected to be there. The men began running as softly as possible across the airfield in search of other aircraft. The aircraft must have been moved, and as the other two planes exploded, they made their way to the RV. Not destroying all the aircraft meant that the remaining aircraft would be used to search for the escaping SAS men.

They met up with the LDRG without incident and made their way across the desert towards Marble Arch. The Germans finally found the SAS patrol on 31 December as they came under attack from a very low flying, twin engine, Messerschmitt Bf 110 fighter. The men below could feel the wash from its two propellers as it whizzed over, opening its two 20mm cannon and strafing them. Lewes was hit in the back and two offside wheels were blown off. One of the SAS soldiers had a piece of shrapnel tear through his shorts, whilst many remarkably got away unscathed. The men jumped out the trucks and made a run for some rocks as the Bf 110 came back around for a second run, with some rounds bouncing off the rocks they were hiding behind. The Bf 110 then made a third run until he had used up all his ammunition and went back to get reinforcements. Lewes was dead, his back semi blown apart and shattered. The men had no choice but to bury him, saying a prayer before scratching his name on a helmet. The other four trucks were soon destroyed by Stuka dive bombers. An LDRG lad inspected the wrecks and said he could get the truck that Lewes was travelling in fixed by taking parts off the wrecked trucks. As dusk approached, they were finally able to make their way back to Jalo. It was a sombre journey, although the men saw in the New Year celebrating with a tin of condensed milk.

Fraser had not had a good time either. They had got into a good position overlooking the airfield, and initially they could not see any aircraft. Then, by the afternoon, the bombers were coming back into the land to refuel and re-arm before taking off again. The defences around the airfield had been strengthened and manned by at least a division of Germans. With no chance of a successful raid, Fraser and his patrol went back to the RV point for the LDRG to come and pick them up. The LDRG were expected by midday on 1 January. By the morning of 2 January 1942, Fraser and his patrol took the assumption that the LDRG would not be turning up to collect them. They were 200 miles away from Jalo and low on water. They had no choice but to march across the desert. They all had a two-day supply of rations and a limited amount of water. Some just sucked pebbles to stop their mouths from drying up. Their luck took a turn for the better when they spotted a lake some miles away from them. That lake turned out to be literally a lifesaver, even though it was salt water and had to be distilled. It took over an hour just to produce a quarter of a pint of drinking water. It tasted foul, especially in a brew, but they had no choice but to drink it. The distilling process needed to continue, but thoughts towards raiding a truck for water and supplies came to the forefront. Two men would carry on distilling while three raided a truck; they drew straws to see who would do what. The raid on a truck was successful, with three of the patrol returning with two Jerry cans of water that turned out to be the most refreshing drinks they had ever had. The next day, with canteens full of water and feeling slightly revived and alert, they made their way towards Jalo, meeting up along the way with some friendly Nomads who offered dates and fresh water. Their only incident was running into some Italian engineers laying cables. They must have thought they were just Italian soldiers; they did not bat an eyelid as the patrol went and hid in some tall grass until nightfall. The plan was to go and raid the truck. Four distinct Italian voices could be heard gabbling away. Fraser made a beeline for the cab and the rest popped open the flap at the rear of the truck, grappling with the men sitting in the back and throwing them out. The Italians begged for mercy and the hope was that their commotion would not cause further investigation from anyone else.

Fraser tried to get some water out of the radiator, but it was an undrinkable mixture of water and rust. They did however find some tins of food, a water bottle and a stove Although it was soon realised that bottle of water contained Benzene for the stove after Du Vivier took a big swig of it and spat it out. They told the Italians to stay quiet as they moved off due east, before moving back due north to ensure they would not be followed if the Italians spilt the beans. The newly acquired stove turned out to be a dud; it blew up the first time it was used for a brew, and the explosion destroyed all their water supply. They continued north until daybreak before finding an area in which to lay up until nightfall. It was close to the coastal road and an ideal ambush site. They decided to ambush a German car containing two Germans. The car was a Mercedes Benz designed for radio use and had three seats in total. The two Germans could not be thrown out, as they would raise the alarm. The five-man patrol squeezed in and, with a revolver to the ear of the German driving the car, they drove past enemy soldiers who did not give the car a second glance. They travelled for over an hour before going off road, where the car became bogged down in a salt marsh and had to be abandoned. The Germans were sent off in one direction with a wish of luck. Fraser and his patrol thought they were now some 40 miles from the British forward positions. What they did not realise at that time was that between them lay Axis defences. They had no choice but to march through them as best they could, avoiding some gun positions and a minefield. Everything went well until they came across some Italian dug-in positions and were spotted by a sentry. The sentry started running away, firing back at them, but in the dark his aim was very poor.

The Italians started to shout; Fraser and his patrol dropped onto their belt buckles and began to crawl for a few hundred feet before standing up and disappearing into the darkness, with the Italians still in some disarray. Early on the next day, the Italian position was bombed by RAF Blenheim Bombers. Fraser and his patrol spent the day within sight of German positions. At nightfall, with rations getting low and feeling very tired, they decided not to make another detour and went straight through the enemy positions. Later, that same night, they came across a Bedouin camp. Again, they were given dates and fresh water, which raised the patrols spirits. By 10 January, they were getting closer, but they were hit by a raging sandstorm, which reduced visibility to almost nil. In the sandstorm, they did not hear or see the armoured column, which thankfully turned out to be British, much to the relief of Fraser and his men. The British, wondering who the hell they were, escorted the men with a bayonet to the CO, looking quite ragged and worse for wear having spent days in the desert without a change of clothes, a wash or a shave. Once they had been confirmed as British soldiers, they were given food and sweet tea to drink to celebrate their rescue. Mayne and his patrol had been much more successful, destroying 27 at Tamit.

Chapter Five

Operation Crusader, after a difficult start, had turned into a successful offensive with Rommel being driven out of Libya. Stirling had taken a plan to Auchinleck to perform a raid on Bouerat, Libya, which was a new Axis base 350 miles west of Benghazi also in Libya. With this, Stirling had been given permission to recruit a further six officers and 40 men. Stirling immediately went about planning the raid. As well as this, he put a recruitment notice up to aid in getting the extra 40 men.

On 21 January 1942, some 36 hours before Stirling was due to raid Bouerat, Rommel launched a counter offensive to regain Benghazi. This meant Bouerat had dropped down in level of importance as the Afika Corps did their best to push the Allies back across the ground they had just taken. Benghazi was then in the hands of the Germans, as was Jalo Oasis and most of Cyrenaica. Stirling still went ahead with his raid on Boureat as it was a pretty much harmless affair. Most of the shipping and supplies being used in Rommel's current offensive had been stripped bare. With the loss of Lewes, Stirling had done a reshuffle and Mayne had been put in place as training officer. Mayne was not happy about his non-operational role and instead of training, he sulked in his tent, even though the training he had undertaken was good. Stirling promised to never give him a non-operational role again. Some of what the SAS had learnt already was being passed on to other branches of the British forces, including the fact that when blowing the wings off of an aeroplane, they would only blow off the right or the left one on each aircraft as they knew the Axis would not have enough spare left wings to repair all the damage. Smashing the dashboard of an aircraft was a good way of disabling it, and again they would only have a limited number of dashboards. Another more unpleasant way was to put a charge and 24-hour pencil fuse into the pilot's seat, hoping it would explode with the pilot in the aircraft.

For Stirling, March 1942 became a bit of a frustrating month. They had undertaken a series of raids against airfields in the

Benghazi area, with 23 aircraft destroyed. Stirling had yet to destroy an aircraft, coming up empty again on his last raid. He decided to lead a raid in Benghazi to blow up shipping. A total of seven of them met with no resistance getting into Benghazi. They had brought a canoe, but it was missing a vital part and could not be used. This continued Stirling's bad luck, although he was convinced that due to how quiet Benghazi was, another raid would be worthwhile. It was two months later, on a moonless night towards the end of May, when Stirling returned to Benghazi, along with Randolph Churchill, the son of Prime Minister Winston Churchill. Randolph had joined 'L' Detachment in April but had not been a suitable candidate as he was overweight. Stirling and Randolph's father were close, so they put him through the training anyway, commenting that although he was losing weight, he was still putting it back on in the evenings.

As for the raid on Benghazi, it turned to be as fruitless as the one in March. The two inflatable boats had leaks. Whilst trying to inflate them, the Italian guards were alerted, and they had to bluff their way out of what they were doing. Stirling decided the next operation was a series of simultaneous airfield raids he had proposed to Auchinleck. The raids were due to be undertaken on 13 June. This raid was Stirling's most ambitious yet; he would take Cooper and Seekings to raid Benna Airfield and Mayne, along with a French party, and they would hit Berka Satellite. All these airfields were within a few miles of Benghazi. Another patrol was French, led by Lieutenant Jacquier, who was tasked with attacking Barce some 60 miles northeast of Benghazi. Finally, a submarine was used by Captain Berge and Jellicoe with another three men to attack Heraklion airfield on Crete. The most daring raid was given to Jordan, a relatively new officer to 'L' Detachment, who would attack airfields in Martuba and Derma with a patrol comprising fifteen Frenchmen from 'L' Detachment and ten SIG (Special Interrogation Group) led by Captain Herbert Buck. Buck had managed to get two lorries, a VW and an Opel car for the raid. All the vehicles had belonged to the Afrika Corps. Jordan and his men would hide in the lorries whilst Buck and his men, disguised as German soldiers, would drive them between the airfields. They left on 8 June and were escorted by the LRDG for the first 200 miles, until they were about 50 miles away from Derna. They were due to RV back at the same location in a week's time. The patrol now managed to travel through two checkpoints (one Italian and one German) without an issue. Later, Jordan and Buck carried out a reconnaissance of Derna and noticed some Bf 110s sitting on the airfield as prime targets. They also noticed 12 Stuka dive-bombers on the Derna east side airfield. Jordan left with his men to carry out the raid later that night. One lorry with four men left for Martuba airfield; another lorry left to attack east and west Derna. The lorry was struggling and kept spluttering to a halt; it took them an hour to cover the six miles to the airfield perimeter.

Once on the airfield, a SIG operative named Hass, decided to go and ask for a spanner from the nearby hanger. The odd German was now around the lorry and when Jordon stuck his head out to see what was going on, he was grabbed and pulled out. It was not long before the lorry was surrounded by agitated Germans. One by one, they all got out of the lorry, less Hass, who was a German Jew and knew his fate already. With the lorry being full of weapons and explosives, he decided to fire his machine gun at the Germans. This in turn caused them to return fire, which caused the lorry to erupt into a ball of fire. The heat started cooking the rounds off, and exploding bullets started to fire in all directions. Jordan got away, after the two Germans holding him dropped to the floor. He waited at the perimeter for ten minutes to see if any others had managed to flee. Sadly, they had not. The rest of the men were sent to POW (Prisoner of War) camps, and seven of them drowned when the prisoner ship, they were travelling in was sunk by British torpedoes. Three managed to escape a POW camp and returned to the SAS in Europe. It was a bitter blow. At the RV, Jordan explained to Bruckner what had happened, but he seemed very nonchalant about it. He must have tipped the Germans off, but there was no point cutting him loose as he knew too much.

This betrayal would affect the other raids as well, as the other airfields were put on a heightened state of alert. As Jacquier's patrol got close to Barce airfield, all the lights went on as if they had been waiting for them. They still managed to blow up a petrol dump on their return to the RV and awaiting LRDG. Six aircraft were destroyed at Berka Main airfield. However, they went in an hour before the other patrol to plant their bombs. The subsequent explosions alerted the Germans, and the other patrol became trapped in fire coming from both ends of the runway. The other patrol had no choice but to hide in ditches, with German soldiers fanning out in search of them. At sunrise, they split up, heading for the Benghazi Escarpment, before finally regrouping and heading to the RV. When Mayne got to the RV, Stirling was already there. He was slightly gleeful that he had finally had a successful raid on the maintenance depot at Benina. Cooper had gone into the hanger with Stirling and placed a bomb on a Bf 110, but Stirling told him to remove it as it was 'his plane' and told him to place it on the Ju-52 a three-engine transport plane. They went into another two hangers and, on passing the guardhouse, Stirling opened the door and tossed in a grenade before running off into the night and hearing the explosion behind them. Stirling got a real kick out of the raid and asked Mayne if he wanted to go back and see the damage he had caused. Stirling, along with Mayne, Cooper, Seekings, Storie and a Palestinian Jewish fellow called Karl, made their way back to Benina. In many respects, it was quite a mad thing to do, to return to the scene of the crime which would by now be very hot and on a high state of alert. They made it through the first roadblock, but Stirling knew the Germans would be on a heightened state of alert. He decided to return home. As Mayne pulled off onto the desert, Stirling spotted a well-lit building a few hundred feet further on. Storie noticed it was a café with German and Italian soldiers enjoying a drink. They drew up alongside it and opened fire, just like a drive-by shooting. The soldiers did not have time to return fire and the café was blown to bits.

Stirling arrived back at Siwa on 21 June, followed a few hours later by Jordan and Buck. The French contingent ran to greet them and as the dust settled, noticed Jordan was crying, feeling full of despair. 21 June was also the day that the Allies hit rock bottom in the desert war. Tobruk has surrendered to Rommel. Rommel had now made three swift advances since the start of his new offensive. Siwa was now in danger and 'L' Detachment needed to evacuate with the LRDG. Stirling went back to Cairo to sort out his next mission and sent his men back to Kabrit in Egypt. By the end of June 1942, the Germans had been halted at El Alamein.

Chapter Six

In Cairo, Egypt, Stirling did his usual round of seeing what he could get. This time he had managed to get 15 American Jeeps, along with 12 Vickers K machine guns from some obsolete Gloster Gladiator Biplanes. He then sweet-talked REME (Royal Electrical and Mechanical Engineers) into mounting the guns fore and aft on the Jeeps. Initially the jeeps were seen by the men as toys, but they soon became the SASs saviours. They were strong and versatile, carrying everything needed on patrol. REME modified the jeeps further to make the suspension stronger and fitted a water condenser to the radiator. The Jeeps only lasted one or two missions, though, as the strain on the engine and gearboxes from climbing massive sand dunes and driving across the desert usually finished them off. In the Gulf War, the SAS used a modified Land Rover to good effect in the Iraqi desert, performing intelligence operations and seeking out Scud missile launchers. Pretty much all the men were not used to driving a Jeep, never mind taking it off road, so they were all given a crash course on how to use the gearbox and 4x4 system, and general off-road handling.

The Afrika Corps starting to flounder and pushed slowly back as Rommel's supply lines had been pushed to near breaking point, so Stirling knew he had a vulnerability. This led him to plan his next operation. On 3 July 1942, the most experienced left Kabrit, before Stirling attacked some forward German airfields on 7 July. Stirling set up a patrol base at Qaret Tartura in Egypt. From there, they would move 60 miles through the German rear lines and towards the airfields. One patrol went to attack Sidi Barrani; another was sent to strafe the coastal road. Fraser and Jordan went to attack two Fuka airfields and Stirling and Mayne headed for Bagoush. Mayne then led his patrol on foot initially to plant their bombs. Some of the bombs failed to go off, so Stirling decided to try a new method. This new method meant driving the Jeep at about 15mph, whilst the Vickers machine gun was fired at the aircraft and caused the Fiat CR42 Biplanes to burst into flames. The only downside was that after three magazines, the Vickers machine gun overheated and started to seize. In the end, 37 planes were destroyed at Bagoush. It took the Germans by surprise, and it was not until the Jeeps were making their way back down the runway that they opened fire. The smoke from the burning planes gave them a degree of cover. Stirling's Jeep had a round penetrate the cylinder head, causing the engine to seize, so they hopped onto another Jeep. The only casualty was a young 21-year-old, John Robson, who had been shot in the head. With the remaining Jeeps, a mile past the perimeter, Stirling called a halt. It was two hours until first light and it would be best if they split into three parties as they headed for the RV. The biggest worry with these raids was not the raids themselves but escaping the often very annoyed Axis forces that would try to pursue them at all costs.

Meanwhile, Jordan and Fraser's patrol drove to within a few miles of the Fuka airfields before covering the final distance on foot. Three stayed behind with the Jeeps and were told to shine a torch at ten-minute intervals from 2-3am to act as a beacon that the patrols could follow as a vector. Fraser returned to the RV at 0230 having found the airfield defences too strong. Jordan's patrol had been more successful, destroying eight planes. They had found the defences strong as well and had been challenged by an Italian Sentry. Jordan spoke to him in German and was let through. Once on the airfield, they followed the tried and tested procedure of planting Lewes bombs underneath the wings in the shadows of each Bf 109 fighter. They were set with ten-minute time delay fuses. After six bombs, had been planted, the Italians finally realised they were under attack and started to fire rounds off in all directions, with none of them effective (although one bullet did hit one of the patrols in the hand). Two more bombs were attached before they withdraw back to the RV.

Of the original 55 men who had been part of 'L' Detachment's first raid, only 16 of them remained. It was early August and 'L' Detachment had been ordered back from the desert. Stirling, on arrival in Cairo, had found out that Churchill had sacked Auchinleck and replaced him with General Alexander, although this did not have an impact on 'L' Detachments next mission.

The Eighth Army was now well entrenched along the El Alamein line, with Montgomery planning a major offensive to start by the end of October. With his supply lines stretched, Montgomery felt that in the short term, Rommel could advance no further. The main concern was Axis supplies coming in via Italian convoys and landing in the ports of Tobruck and Benghazi. Stirling had been given orders to lead a large-scale assault on Benghazi. He already had two failed attempts under his belt, and this third one horrified him. He had 200 men, half of whom came from other units. They were all transported over a thousand miles from Cairo in a convoy of 80 vehicles, along with two Honey tanks, otherwise known as the M3 Stuart American light tank. However, after about ten miles, the two tanks broke down.

'L' Detachment started to leave Kufta Oasis - Mayne first on 4 September, and then Cumper on 5 September, heading out with their convoy to an RV in the Jebel Mountains. On 6 September, Stirling left Kufta for his 800-mile trek across the desert. Desert navigation is never easy with often very few reference points to go by. The best method was to stick religiously to the bearings, not let doubt creep in and start making adjustments. On 11 September, all three patrols were in the RV. Stirling had heard that an Arab spy had stated that there was now a German Battalion in the Northeast of the city and some 5000 Italian soldiers scattered around Benghazi. Stirling contacted MEHQ in Cairo and was told by his commanders that it was just 'gossip' and to ignore it.

The convoy of jeeps and lorries left just as the sun was setting on 13 September, although all did not go according to plan. The guide got them lost on the approach to Benghazi, which meant the diversionary raid laid on by the RAF was over before they had made it to the harbour in Benghazi. Driving without lights made it even harder, so Stirling ordered lights to be turned on, instantly making the convoy recognisable to the enemy. At 0430, they came to a roadblock with a pillar box just further down the road. The pillar box would need to be taken out before the convoy could progress. Almonds took his jeep down the road, and both sides of the road instantly opened up on the Jeep and the convoy. The Vickers guns on Almonds' Jeep opened up and silenced the Italians for a few seconds. Stirling gave the order to retreat to the relative safety of the escarpment before dawn. The fast retreat meant the convoy became broken up as the Jeeps and lorries retreated as quickly as they could, knowing that planes may well be sent up to strafe and bomb them. The men made it about 12 miles before they were attacked. Everyone was jumping off the various Jeeps and lorries as the first fighter attacked. Boutinot managed to jump off his Jeep just in time before it exploded under a hail of bullets. Lack of cover was the biggest issue, and they knew only luck was going to get them out of this scrape.

They were still 25 miles away from the RV. With the attack over, they had to either cling onto the remaining Jeeps and lorries or walk. They had lost 12 vehicles in total and suffered a few fatalities. Any badly wounded had to be left where they fell as Stirling, Seekings and Cooper went out to look for stragglers. Over the next couple of days, what was left of the convoy arrived back at the RV. At the RV, a further four seriously wounded had to be left, including a REME fitter who had volunteered to look after the vehicles and saw it as a great learning opportunity. Sadly, all four of the men died in captivity.

This setback was offset on 28 September when Stirling was told that 'L' Detachment was to expand to regimental size. At the time, regimental size was set at 29 officers and 572 other ranks. Stirling quickly filled up the spaces he had before preparing the regiment for the next mission for what was the now 1st SAS Regiment with four squadrons, a general squadron, a Free French squadron, a Greek squadron, and the SBS (Special Boat Section). A squadron moved to a base in the Great Sand Sea, attacking the railway line as the countdown to the El Alamein offensive began on 23 October. With the Germans in retreat, the SAS spent their time on the coastal road shooting up Germans, blowing up lorries and laying mines.

One patrol, led by one of the new officers, McDermott, was on its way back to base when it got a bit too close to a Flack 88 battery, which was a German anti-aircraft and anti-tank artillery gun that fired 88mm rounds. The first they knew of it was when an armour-piercing round tore the front of one of the three Jeeps the patrol had. The Jeep's engine and bonnet had been completely torn off and lay somewhere in the desert. The other two Jeeps accelerated off as quickly as they could, leaving the immobilised Jeep and its men behind. The four men had no choice but to walk out of the desert. After a day and a half of walking and seeing, no other SAS patrols, they decided to head for the coastal road and try to ambush a German vehicle. A German Luftwaffe truck found them first after shouting at them in Italian, prompting Storie to wave back at them. They soon realised they were British but assumed they were shot down RAF crew rather than SAS, as they did not wear any insignia on operations. The Germans in the truck treated them well as they headed back towards some defensive positions at El Aghellia, although the Americans were advancing fast east and their first Army would soon link up with the Eighth Army moving west.

Chapter Seven

'A' Squadron left their base on the Great Sand Sea in Egypt, to establish a new base at Bit Zelten, Libya and 'B' Squadron came and joined them on 29 November 1942. Now, many of the men were starting to get concerned about Stirling. He did not look a healthy man; he had sores, which had been caused by the sand getting into open wounds. This caused an infection that would often lead to an eruption of pus and subsequent hospitalisation. The other major affliction the men got was from sand getting into their goggles and the sun's glare and the fine white sand causing solar conjunctivitis. Stirling also became increasingly overworked while Mayne was out in the desert. He had taken on the training of B Squadron, as well as pushing through the setting up of a second SAS regiment. The SBS Squadron would also fall under his command, and he had a new influx of Free French recruits to train.

When Mayne returned, Stirling told him of his operation for the forthcoming month. It was a simple concept that 'A 'Squadron would shoot up any enemy vehicles between Sirte and El Agheila, whilst 'B' Squadron would move 200 miles west to destroy targets in Libya around Tripoli.

However, the raids by 'B' Squadron would prove costly, with many men either being killed or taken as POWs. Stirling was still congratulated by Montgomery for what the SAS had achieved so far. His next plan was to carry out reconnaissance patrols in north Tunisia whilst destroying the Axis lines of communication and becoming the first unit to link up with the advancing First Army. Stirling's first problem was getting enough petrol for the raid; it needs to be sourced and collected.

At dawn on 15 January 1943, Stirling led a patrol consisting of eight Jeeps and headed west towards Ghadames. The going was difficult, with the soft sand and high dunes. Rocks started to shred the tyres as they were not up to the sort of terrain they were driving on; other Jeeps had to be cannibalised to keep other Jeeps going. On 21 January, the patrols met up at an RV a few miles south of Bir Soltane in Tunisia. Stirling had learnt that

Gafsa and Tripoli had been recaptured. This meant that they needed to attack the Axis lines of communication between Gabes and Sfax as a priority. Jordan departed at 4pm, heading for Gabes Gap some 80 miles north. Stirling would then follow-on 22 January, 12 hours later. Jordon realised he needed to reach his area of operations before dawn, but that soon became difficult with the loss of the sun compass. Even at night, navigating by the stars and the huge sand dunes slowed the Jeeps down to a walking pace. Radio contact was also hit and miss. In one area, it could be almost crystal clear, and then in another it was impossible to get any form of signal. It had taken them 24 hours to travel 30 miles and they still had another 50 miles to go. The terrain was even worse than had been the case the night before, when their luck suddenly changed, and they found a road. The Jeeps could open up on the road and travel at 40mph for nearly an hour before they saw some oncoming vehicles. These vehicles had German markings. The jeeps moved to the far right to try to drive past them. Jordan swerved his Jeep away from an armoured car and were bogged down in the sand at the side of the road.

The armoured car stopped, and a German soldier emerged from the turret, his eyes meeting Jordan's. All Jordan could do was change gears to get out of the sand and then accelerate down the road before the armoured car had a chance to fire. He finally let off a few rounds at the seventh and final Jeep, disabling it. The jeeps roared off into the desert only to run into three German lorries, and rather than flee, Jordan decided to fight. During the confusion of the firefight, the radio Jeep became separated from the rest of the patrol, ended up in a ditch and was out of action. Another Jeep was lost during the firefight, bringing the total number of Jeeps down to four, having lost five since the start of the patrol. The four Jeeps finally passed through Gabes Gap on 24 January.

The next day, Jordan and his patrol began to lay mines on the routes from Sfax to Gabes. On the evening of 25 January, a skirmish with an armoured car split the patrol in two. Jordon tried to locate them and was stopping to ask a shepherd as a section of Italian soldiers came into view on a ridge. As they carried heavy machine guns, they had no choice but to surrender. Another patrol, led by Martin had made it through the gap and could lay explosives on the stretch of railway line between Gabes and Gafsa. They also mined the road that ran alongside the track before withdrawing half a mile to watch a train blow up, followed by a staff car and motorcycle escort as it drove over a mine. The next evening, their luck started to run out when the local Arabs told the Germans about their position. As the German patrol approached, they blew up the Jeeps with a pre-installed Lewes bomb to ensure they did not fall into enemy hands. Martin and his patrol then ran away and spent the next three days walking towards Gafsa, making use of their emergency rations. They were picked up on 30 January by an American unit and initially held as POWs until their identities could be verified.

  Stirling, following in the tyre tracks of Jordan, also realised that the schedule he had put in place was unachievable due to the terrain. It was as hard on the men, as it was on the Jeeps traversing the harsh terrain. Stirling made it to Gabes Gap in the early hours of 23 January and was then spotted by a German Fi-156 high wing monoplane spotter plane. Stirling still managed to get through safely and by the next morning, they were on the road travelling west to Gsfsa. As they travelled down the road, a German armoured column was spotted parked up on either side. Stirling and his patrol simply drove straight past them, looking straight ahead, as they lay about on their armoured vehicles drinking coffee. As they got further down the road, enemy activity increased, and Stirling decided to get off the road and head north cross country to find a place to lay up and rest. The whole patrol fell asleep without posting any sentries, only to be awoken by two Afrika Corps soldiers standing over them. The soldiers motioned for them to stay where they were, but that was not an option; as soon as they moved forward, a few of the patrol got up and ran like hell. As soon as they ran, the German soldiers started screaming their heads off and were joined by more soldiers. Only Sadler, Cooper and Taxis had managed to get away. The other eleven, including Stirling, were being bundled into the back of some lorries and taken away. The three, left behind were also in a difficult position, deep behind enemy lines with no weapons, food or water. Cooper had a map at least and they began to march towards a large salt lake called Djerid. They knew the French were at Tozeur on the north side of the lake.

They managed to get some water and dates from some Arabs. They later ran into a not-quite-so-friendly tribe of Berbers who demanded their clothes, and as the three men ran away rocks were thrown at them. Cooper was hit by a rock and his forehead started to bleed profusely. They continued to march through the night and found another kind Arab woman who gave them some more water and dates to keep them going. Their boots and feet were getting into an increasingly worse state. Hallucinations also began to set in as dehydration took hold. They finally saw some buildings, but the hallucinations meant that they were not sure if they were real. Sure enough, they had made it to Tozeur and into the arms of the French.

With the loss of Stirling, the SAS had been dealt a bitter blow. Stirling would spend the rest of the war at Colditz. This was not the end of the SAS, however, as they had proven their worth in North Africa and now their attentions would be set on Sicily and Italy.

Chapter Eight
Sicily 1943

2SAS were camped a few miles east of Philippeville, a coastal town in Algeria. 2SAS was being commanded by David Stirling's brother, Bill Stirling. 2SAS had already carried out a few raids in Jeeps in front of the First Army's advance through Algeria and Tunisia. Bill Stirling, however, just like his brother, wanted to plan bigger and more strategically important operations. Bill Stirling also saw the importance of parachute operations, even after his brother's ill-fated first parachute operation. Training was still intense to ensure all recruits were up to the required standard. Improvisations were made to allow an assortment of training. One idea was to use a light railway wagon, push it to the top of the hill, and then ride back down the hill and jump out to practice being able to roll and land whilst moving. It was an activity not without its dangers, and it did cause some serious injuries. Bill Stirling was a much less hands-on officer than his brother and spent more time at HQ than with his regiment. David Stirling was a more physical and charismatic individual. However, he, like his brother, had the ability to handle people and gain the admiration of the men he was commanding.

The war in North Africa was declared over on 12 May 1943 and preparations were made for the invasion of Sicily. This included Special Forces and the SBS which, after the capture of David Stirling, had seen 1SAS split into two squadrons. The SBS under Lord Jellicoe and SRS (Special Reconnaissance Service) under Mayne meant that 1SAS had temporarily ceased to exist. The SBS was training in Plastine initially, until Jellicoe brought the SBS to Philippeville. The SBS were to later carry out some diversionary raids on Sardinia that would be carried out with the invasion of Sicily on 10 July 1943.

Bill Stirling had planned a raid on Lampedusa that was currently being held by the Italians. The island was 75 miles east of Tunisia and is the largest island of the Italian Pelagie Islands in the Mediterranean Sea. The raid's objective was to destroy a radar station located on top of a cliff. The raid was planned for the end of May and not all the factors had been considered. For example, the radar station would be able to pick up the incoming raiders on their MTBs (Motor Torpedo Boat). The raiders transferred to canoes half a mile from the shore and paddled towards the shore. Not far from the shore, the canoes were spotted by the cliff-top searchlight and had to withdraw as small arms fire started to rain down on them. This was followed by artillery shells as fountains of water started to sprout up between the canoes, until one canoe was hit. The MTBs, seeing what was happening, moved in closer to pick up the men in the canoes. Amazingly, everyone escaped.

Bill Stirling was still trying to get 2SAS to be used strategically as opposed to in support of a larger operation. In the end, he was instructed to carry out two operations during the initial landings on Sicily. The first was Operation Narcissus, which would involve 50 men making a beach assault to attack a lighthouse on the southeast coast of Sicily, which was reported to have guns installed that could disrupt the main landing. The other was Operation Chestnut, which was more to Bill Stirling's liking. The idea was to parachute in with ten men to Northern Sicily to carry out a range of raids sabotaging enemy communications, rail and roads. Bill Stirling thought that neither raid would really help raise the profile of the SAS. Operation Chestnut did not go according to plan; the men ended up being dispersed over a wide area, rations were lost, and radios damaged on landing. One of the two officers leading the raid, Captain Bridgeman-Evans, got himself captured. The other, Operation Narcissus, was a success though; the lighthouse was captured without a single casualty. However, no concealed guns were found at the lighthouse and only three Italian soldiers were guarding it. The raid had ended up with just 13 men from the proposed 50, mainly due to the high number of cases of malaria being suffered by soldiers. Bill Stirling took Operation Chestnut as a learning curve, and this was relayed back to HQ in his report.

On 9 July 1943, the SRS under Mayne had been further subdivided into three troops, which were then divided into three sections. Each section had one officer and 20 men. One, Two and Three Troop were due to land by assault craft on the south coast of Sicily. One Troop would head for some guns on the northern side and Two Troop would launch an assault on a series of buildings to the west of their landing. Three Troop, meanwhile, would move inland to capture a strategic objective that would cut the road leading to the guns. The journey across the sea had been a difficult one, with rough seas making many of the men quite sick. At 1am on 10 July, the order was given for the SRS to get ready. The men then moved out onto the LCAs (Landing Craft Assault), bobbing up and down violently on the choppy sea. The beach was about half a mile away. In the sea between them and the beach where several Airspeed Horsa gliders, with men still clinging onto them. The LCAs picked up a few, but many had to be left behind to fight for their lives in the sea. They had been part of an airborne force of some 137 gliders, but the gliders had been released too early and 47 had ended up in the sea.

At around 0300, the first LCA hit the beach and the men jumped over, before running up the beach and scaling a cliff. There was no enemy fire raining down on them; if anything, it was eerily quiet until they heard mortar fire, scoring a direct hit onto a gun battery's ammo dump and the whole thing exploding. Two Troop had landed half a mile east further than planned, which had put them in the most dangerous position, right below the gun battery. However, they were not coming under any form of fire and the only gun they could hear was a Bren gun being used by commanded One Troop by Fraser. One Troop had not been content with just capturing a few buildings and decided to attack the same gun battery as Two Troop. One of One Troop's sections, led by Wiseman, used the mortar fire and good use of dead ground right up to the perimeter of the gun positions. As soon as the mortar fire had finished, he went straight in, taking the enemy by surprise and wounding, killing and capturing 40 enemy soldiers. Wiseman, for his actions, earned a Military Cross. The Italians seemed to have lost the will to fight and were much happier just to surrender. The greatest danger was from what we now call 'blue on blue,' or friendly fire incidents, with Troops having landed in the wrong places. Two Troop did indeed come under fire from One Troop until they shouted "Desert Rats" in an attempt to make them realise who they were.

One of Two Troops sections led by Harrison, who was escorting engineers to the guns to blow them up, came under fire from what must have been a friendly gun; it was firing red tracer rounds rather than the green ones used by the Italians. Thankfully, none of the bullets from the Bren gun hit anyone and Harrison could establish that they were a friendly force. At dawn, Harrison's section, along with the engineers, reached the gun battery. The engineers went to inspect the guns, which turned out to be British guns from the end of the First World War. The guns were dealt with by opening the breech and placing a charge across the hinges of the breech. The subsequent explosion and twisted metal put the guns out of action.

At 5:20am, Mayne fired off a flare from a Very pistol to signal to the invasion fleet that the guns had been blown. As the fleet of ships approached, a second gun battery opened up inland. One, Two and Three Troop marched up to a farm that had been the strategic objective to cut off the road to the gun battery to formulate a plan. The farm was also a holding area for all the Italian POWs.

With a plan in place, One, Two and Three Troop moved on to the next gun battery, leaving a few soldiers behind to guard the prisoners. On route to the object, Harrison's section came across what looked like seven unarmed Italians. As they got to within 150 feet, the seven Italians dropped to the floor and opened up small arms fire on Harrison's section. Another section led by Seekings had had the same done to them, only this time one of Seekings' section, Canton, had been shot in the thigh. A very angry Seekings stormed their position, killing all of them. After that, Seekings went on to destroy a pillar box with grenades before finally killing the occupants with his revolver. He won a military medal for his actions.

Contact from the Italians was sporadic but could also be quite effective. Finally, they made it to the second gun battery, which was captured quite easily. Once again, accurate mortar fire had taken out their ammo dump. The engineers did not have enough explosives left to damage them so had to manually do so by ensuring they could not be moved up, down, left or right. There had only been one fatality during the whole operation and that was Canton, who had been shot in the leg and died from loss of blood sometime later, before reaching hospital.

Both gun batteries had been destroyed, leaving the invasion fleet safe to land. 150 enemy soldiers had been killed and a further 500 captured. The prisoners were later handed over to the Fifth Division.

Chapter Nine

Augusta in Sicily was an important naval port and needed to be captured as soon as possible. The city is situated in Syracuse and faces the Ionian Sea. The old town is an island, made by cutting an isthmus in the 16th century and is connected to the mainland by two bridges. A white flag had been seen flying above the town's citadel, which seemed to suggest the town had been evacuated. The plan was to land the SRS from a ship called *Monarch*, which would sail directly into the harbour before offloading the SRS into landing craft. Augusta was seen as an important strategic objective which the Eight Army could use to continue their advance north. What the SRS were not aware of, was that the high ground area above Augusta was still occupied by the German Battle Group Schmatz. At 4:30am on 12 July 1943, the destroyer *Eskimo* had been badly damaged by enemy fire. The heavy and sustained fire had driven away the ships following *Eskimo*. HMS *Eskimo* was a Tribal-class destroyer, laid down by the High Walker Yard of Vickers Armstrong at Newcastle-on-Tyne on 5 August 1936. She was launched on 3 September 1937 and commissioned on 30 December 1938. She was later used as a target ship in the Gareloch, before being sold for scrap on 27 June 1949 and finally broken up at Troon in Cornwall.

The SRS attack had been planned to be undertaken in two waves; the first wave would see One and Three Troop land first, before the landing craft went back to pick up Two Troop and a Mortar team. As soon as One and Three Troop had landed, Three Troop was to make its way straight through the town before crossing the bridge and capturing the railway station. It would finally come to a halt a mile outside of Augusta and hold the line, until being relieved by 17 Brigade advanced party. The raid was due to begin at 1930 and speed was of the essence. As the first landing craft got within a quarter of a mile, the Germans opened up on them and the beach area was under heavy fire. Destroyers opened up on the German positions and scored a few direct hits. Three Troop jumped off the landing craft and made their way up the beach. As they hit the beach, they came under heavy small arms fire and took the first casualties. Three Troop continued up through the town, followed by One Troop.

By now, the landing craft had returned to the ship to collect Two Troop. It was not long before Two Troop was running down the ramp trying not to slip on the rocks as bullets ricocheted off them. One soldier was killed not long after stepping off the landing craft ramp. Using the standard street fighting drill of moving doorway to doorway, Two Troop advanced before establishing a base in a public garden. They took up defensive positions in the garden, including setting up a Bren gun. Further ahead Three Troop was probing enemy defences, only coming under sporadic fire and with one casualty as Sgt Frame was shot through the neck. As they crossed the bridge and neared the railway station, they split up, with one section flanking left and one section flanking right, while the third section went straight ahead. By now, it was dark, and with one section huddled up against a dry-stone wall, they saw a patrol of Germans approaching. They allowed them to simply file on by as the Germans seemed to have no idea who they were. When they got about 100 feet away, a Bren gun was opened up on them, killing them all instantly. Another section ran into German machine gun and mortar fire as they carried on up the road after crossing the bridge. They managed to get mortar fire directed by the mortar team that had landed with Two Troop, but it proved ineffective. Three Troop had no choice but to go firm and send a runner back down into the town. There was a growing fear of a counterattack with quite intense and heavy fire that could lead to casualties. Three Troop came under heavy fire, a tank joined in and a PIAT (Projector, Infantry, Anti-Tank) MK1 was fired at the tank, hitting the frontal armour and just bouncing off. This led Three Troop into a retreat to the railway station. The cunning Germans rang the railway station's telephone and when Three Troop answered, started to rain artillery shells down on it. Ammunition was running low, and radios had been damaged by salt water, which meant the squadron's signaller could not call in for artillery support from the destroyers. Worse still was that there was no sign of 17 Brigade either. Mayne had to make the decision to withdraw Three Troop back behind the bridge.

The British Mortar team gave them some cover as they mortared the German mortar positions that were firing on Three Troop. The Germans seemed to advance no further during the night even though tracked vehicle movement could be heard. By morning, 17 Brigade advanced party had made it through and drove past the now deserted German positions before linking up with Three Troop. It had been a close-run operation that could have easily ended in disaster if the Germans had pushed through with a full counterattack.

The SRS spent the rest of July camped at Augusta, enjoying a brief respite and sleeping under olive trees or swimming in the warm Mediterranean Sea. However, they still endured several nights of enemy air attacks. In August, the squadron moved to Cannizzaro and on 17 August, Winston Churchill was informed that the last of 40,000 German soldiers had dispersed, which meant the next objective would be Italy. This meant the squadron needed to get back into a harsh training regime in preparation for the next operation. On 1 September, the SRS moved to Catania. On 4 September, the SRS were attacking the German-held coastal town of Bagnara in southern Italy. They were two and a half hours behind schedule after the 169-foot LCIs (Landing Craft Infantry) ran into problems.

One had become delayed after a propeller jammed and another had run aground. The only alternative was to transfer the SRS to smaller LCAs. As the SRS finally landed, they got off the landing craft and made their way up the beach, keeping a watchful eye for any signs that the beach had been mined. Due to the late landing, the plan had to change; and Two Troop was tasked with pushing forward in a straight line to then hold the bridge in the north of the town. One Troop would seal off the northern approaches to the town and Three Troop would secure the road and railway to the south of the town. Dawn aided the squadrons' move along the streets. One Troop made it to the crossroads some 400 feet inland before moving on towards the bridge, crossing the bridge and pushing past Two Troop. On looking behind him, Davis from One Troop saw what he thought was Three Troop bringing up the rear, but there was something not right about their headgear as he viewed them through binoculars. They were in fact German engineers who were advancing on the bridge to blow it up. They had no realisation that there would be SRS soldiers and got quite a shock when they first realised what they had bumped into. A few were killed almost straight away as a quick ambush was put into action. Those that were not killed made a run for it down the streets. The noise of gunfire however, had alerted the Germans on the high ground overlooking Bagnara. They had no idea that the SRS had made it through. The SRS landing on the northern beach instead of the heavily mined southern beach gave the SRS an initial upper hand.

The Germans had a gun battery on a plateau above the town with a Flak 88 and several 4-inch mortars. The Germans started to open up and One Troop's temporary HQ was hit directly, killing four instantly. Increasing machine gun fire was also poured down onto the bridge. Meanwhile, Three Troop was yet to meet any resistance; all they found in the railway tunnels were scared locals. One Troop was making its way up a road on the hillside, using cover as best as they could. It was a straight section of road, about 350 feet in length, which proved to be more problematic as a machine gun opened up. All they could do was sprint forward, trying to find some cover. In the end, a small cottage provided refuge some 200 feet from the German machine gun position. The position the Germans had chosen was a perfect vantage point overlooking the town and the road leading up the hillside. For the moment, they would have to stay put whilst mortar fire was trained on Two Troop at the bridge. With part of One Troop effectively pinned down and getting frustrated, Davis began to formulate a plan. He would take two others, crawl to the culvert that ran under the road and crawl through it. The moment Tobin, who was going with Davis along with Storey, stepped out of the door, his upper torso was riddled with bullets, and he lay dead. The Germans became more effective with their fire and the cottage's walls were becoming pockmarked. Another bullet hit Tunstall, causing him to bleed profusely from the mouth.

The Germans continued firing for a further 30 minutes before ceasing. Another part of One Troop had heard the firing as they waited in a cutting further down the road and were told to move up to Davis's position. On moving up, they came under quite effective mortar fire and had no choice but to run back the way they had come. The German machine gun then opened up on them, hitting hands and feet initially. Thankfully, no one had been seriously wounded, but they had been lucky to escape with their lives. Davis was trapped in the cottage with his section for a further eight hours, when under the cover of night, they were able to make it back to the rest of One Troop. Then the first piece of good news came in via a runner that 15 Infantry Brigade had reached the town, ready to relive the SRS. The next day, with 15 Infantry, having established itself in the town, a British cruiser moved up, trained its guns on the German battery and opened up. The fearsome firepower from the cruiser was enough to force the Germans to withdraw. This prompted 15 Brigade to advance up the hillside to meet up with One Troop.

Chapter Ten
Italy 1943-1945

The SRS was billeted up at Gallico, Italy only a few miles down the road from Bagnara when the news of the Italian armistice on 8 September 1942 came through. It was time for the squadron to move, leaving on 22 September 1942 and then sailing towards Termoli, a port that was strategically important due to its position to take part in Operation Devon. It had a busy main road that ran laterally across Italy. This road would also help the advance in Naples. The SRS mounted up, on an LCI, and two further LCIs containing 3 Commando and 40 Royal Marine Commando would work alongside them to form the SSB (Special Service Brigade). The sea conditions in the early hours of 3 October were appalling even half a mile from the shore. Instead of swapping to an LCA, the SRS took the LCI all the way in until it became grounded on a sandbank some 100 feet from the shore. The water was too deep to wade meaning the men would have to swim ashore. The first few minutes were full of confusion as the men became mixed up and officers spent time rounding them all up and into their respective units.

One Troop was heading for a bridge, Two Troop was tasked with moving four miles inland and attacking the fleeing German soldiers, while Three Troop were also tasked with capturing a bridge and holding it until they were relieved by the British 78th Division. The commandos were tasked with taking the town itself, and the HQ of the German 1st Parachute Division was soon captured. Such was the speed of the attack, the Germans were taken by surprise and useful, sensitive documents were captured as the Germans did not have enough time to destroy them. The Germans had expected a landing but from the southeast, not the west. The SRS was also making progress; a section from Three Troop shot up a German vehicle, killing one and capturing three. As they moved further inland, they caught up with more of the German withdrawal and started to exchange more fire. They then came across many German soldiers who they assumed were prisoners of war, having been captured by the 78th Division. That realisation was soon lost when they started to fire on the SRS section. They made a hasty retreat backward. One of the SRS soldiers was killed as they tried to escape. Another section from Three Troop came to the rescue and a fierce firefight began. The intense fight finished with another injured SRS soldier, five dead and nine captured German paratroopers. One and Two Troop continued to come across small pockets of resistance, almost as if the Germans were being bloody-minded. A farmhouse containing some German soldiers was mortared and a direct hit was scored on the roof with a HE (High Explosive) round. It fatally wounded one officer and the others appeared from the farmhouse looking rather ragged with ripped uniforms. Two Troop was having great fun raking enemy vehicles with gunfire as the German vehicles tried to flee. By midday on 3rd October, Termoli had been captured. A perimeter was set up around the town by the SRS, 40 Commando with 3 Commando staying in the centre of the perimeter to move up if required. The tally stood at 100 German dead and 150 captured. It had been a very successful operation.

4 October started very peacefully, but that was to change later as the Germans decided to make a counterattack early in the morning on 5 October. This initial German attack with tanks was a diversionary raid. The main attack was launched by 64 and 79 Panzer Grenadiers and attacked the Argyle and Sutherland Highlanders on the high ground around Termoli. They had no choice but to fall back until reinforcements arrived. At 9am, five Sherman tanks from the County of London Yeomanry were sent in to push back the German advance. Four of these were destroyed and the fifth had to withdraw. At 1115, the anti-tank guns of the Highlanders were overrun and retreated further back. Brigadier Howlett was furious and ordered that they must hold the line to the last. The SRS became aware of the attack when a salvo fell behind them; this was followed by German bombers, bombing the harbour. The German tanks were now moving in on their left flank; the counterattack was at its most fierce. Shells had landed directly on 40 Commando positions,

killing and wounding quite a number of them. With no armour support, this was going to be a difficult fight.

The Germans continued to push through and just after 1430; every available SRS man was rushed forward to help push back the advancing attack. They climbed into the back of lorries and just as they were doing so, several shells landed around them, filling the street with black smoke and spreading panic. Several men had shrapnel embedded in them and only the first lorry had been destroyed; the rest looked pretty much intact. An Italian family and several SRS soldiers died during the shelling. The force of the explosion had ripped one SRS soldier to bits with what remained of his head now hanging on the wires from a telegraph pole. One was still at the wheel of a lorry and looked as though he was asleep; a piece of shrapnel had cut him in two. Another SRS soldier was nothing more than charred remains still burning until a bucket of water was thrown over him. The street reeked of the smell of cordite and burnt flesh, along with a strange, sweet smell.

What remained of the SRS did their best to hold back the attack whilst coming under Flak 88 fire and a multi rocket launcher called a Nebelwerfer, which made a strange moaning sound as they flew. By the evening, the SRS was coming under attack from 11 tanks along with around 100 infantry. They had a six-pounder gun as fire support, but this soon got overrun and was left intact, ready for the Germans to use if they so desired.

By nightfall, 3 Commando had managed to repel the attack, even with the Germans still on three sides. The German losses had been heavy, partly due to a well-positioned and expertly aimed Vickers machine gun manned by a detachment of Kensingtons that cut many of the Germans down as they advanced. Earlier on, in the day, 2SAS had arrived with a detachment of 100 men and they quickly moved into position on a lip overlooking the railway goods yard. This gave them a great over watch position; they could see members of 40 Commando unit hiding behind tombstones some 300 feet in front of them. Just after 5pm, three German Tiger tanks began to attack further down the railway line. These were quite formidable tanks. All

2SAS had, was a six-pounder gun and several Bren guns, so knew they were potentially outgunned before they even started any form of attack. All 2SAS could do was open up with everything they had and continue to lay down a very large number of rounds. The SAS dragged another two six pounders into position, and this surprisingly made the Tiger Tanks back off. With the railway line now the new point of attack, a section of SRS came to join them. Later, in the night, the Germans tried again to break through the railway yard, but 2SAS held them off and pushed them back again. They were getting low on ammo and so when the Germans retreated after getting about 500 feet from their position, was a great relief to 2SAS.

The next morning at first light, a couple of Bf 110 fighters swooped low over the SAS positions to be shortly followed by a squadron of Spitfires who chased them off. Despite the heavy shelling and loss of life, the SRS spirits were still quite high. What lifted their spirits the most was the news that 38 Irish Brigade had landed and were preparing for a large assault. The Irish brought a much-needed supply of ammunition as the Germans continued to attack the cemetery where 40 Commando were still holed up. They came under mortar fire and had to retreat, then as soon as the Germans moved forward, they were also mortared into retreat. At around midday, word started to spread that the Germans had begun to pull back. The SRS and 40 Commando seized the opportunity and pushed up towards a ridge some 400 feet ahead of their current position. Finally, at a quarter to three in the afternoon, the Irish regiment began their offensive and pushed the Germans further back.

The past 36 hours had been a big strain on the SRS and their faces told the story of what they had been through. The SRS had taken the heaviest casualties with 21 killed, 24 wounded and 24 missing. 40 Commando had six killed and 30 wounded, and 3 Commando had five killed and 29 wounded. The Allied losses had been heavy, but the Germans laid defeated, and many brave and heroic acts had been shown when facing superior numbers and firepower.

The SRS stayed for a further week in Termoli and it was a wet and reflective experience for many. The SRS found out that the church tower had been used as a forward observation post for the artillery and was the reason it had been so deadly accurate. On 12 October 1943, the SRS set off for Molfetta and were happy to leave the horrors of Termoli behind. 2SAS had been busy up to Termoli with a successful operation under their belt (this was Operation Speedball, the aim of which had been to blow up a railway tunnel). Several other railway tunnels were blown, along with the sabotaging of railway lines. Such was the disruption they were causing that a division of Austrian mountain troops were brought in to track them down. It was hard living, surviving on what the forest had to offer. In total, they spent some 112 days on the operation and all the survivors lost several stones in weight.

Christmas and New Year 1943 came and went, and it was soon 1944. 2SAS were given the go-ahead to undertake two operations that had been cancelled in December. The targets were two railway lines in Rimini and Ancona. The hope was that this would severely disrupt supply lines. It was called Operation Thistledown and was a success, with 25 vehicles destroyed and one train derailed over a ten-day period. However, everyone was captured. The second operation, Operation Driftwood, was to attack mainly rail targets north of Rome. They managed to destroy a railway line before all men went missing after boarding a six and half metre boat in the south sea of Porto San Girgio. They were never seen again and no trace of them ever found. It is believed they may have been sunk by Allied aircraft patrolling the area.

On 12 January 1944, 2SAS went back to their roots slightly as they were tasked with attacking aircraft at an airfield at San Agidio. This was known as Operation Pomegranate. A six-man party was dropped in by parachute near Perugia, although, both officers leading the raid became separated from the other four in the raiding party. The two officers made it to San Egidio airfield and placed bombs on the seven-aircraft present. A spare one exploded, killing one of the officers, Widdington; the second officer, Hughes, was captured and later escaped. The other four SAS soldiers made no attempt to attack the enemy and were all RTU'd.

The last mission of the Sicily and Italy campaign for 2SAS was a strategic railway bridge south of Pesaro that linked the coastal line between Rimini and Ancona. In late January, a detachment of 2SAS made their way on a destroyer to their dropping-off point. Laws and Dowell, two of the eight-man raiding party, used canoes to make it to shore before scaling a cliff and spending a night in a cave. On 30 January, Laws and Dowell went out to recce the bridge and found it quite heavily guarded. They also investigated a house to see if it was being used as a barracks by the Italians. They found it to contain 19 soldiers, so they decided that between them they would place a large rock on the door to slow down the Italian soldiers' exit. At 1115, Laws sent a signal to the raiding part to make way to the bridge. The six men, complete with plastic explosives, got into a boat and made their way to the shore. One man was left with the boat, whilst the other five men went and joined Laws and Dowell.

They found that there was not a single guard on the bridge, which made it almost too easy to place the charges on key points along the bridge to ensure it collapsed. The charges had a ten-minute fuse and once they had all been placed, the seven men ran away as fast as their legs could carry them. The Italians had finally realised something was going on and were trying to get out to fire upon the raiders. They all made it to the boat and canoes before any ineffective fire started and by the time, they had made it about 500 feet out to sea, the small arms fire stopped. From the boats, they could see the Italian soldiers searching for the explosives and after ten minutes, the charges had not gone off. After 12 minutes, there was an explosion that sent a few Italian soldiers flying through the air and severely damaged the bridge. It took the Germans a week to repair the bridge.

Chapter Eleven

Thirty-three men of 2SAS parachuted into Northern Italy on 27 December 1944 to conduct Operation Galia. The idea of Operation Galia was that 3SAS would make the Germans believe a much larger force of around 400 had parachuted in. They would parachute in behind the advancing Germans and then attack the main supply routes. They had landed near a small village in the mountains called Rossano. The SAS soldiers endured quite hard landings and became quite scattered, losing quite a few of the supply containers dropped with them. They would have the help of two very different groups of Italian partisans - one anti-fascist and pro Allies, and the other communist and wanting to store up as many weapons as they could, ready for a revolution after the war was over. To help with dealing with the two very different groups, they had an SEO officer. The men were divided into three separate teams, which were further divided up into patrols. These patrols would then fan out across the area of operations and make their way into the valley, attacking enemy transport and enemy positions whilst maintaining a great amount of activity to fool the Germans into thinking a much bigger force was involved. As in the rest of Europe, Italy was in the clutches of one of the coldest winters in living memory. The clothing the SAS had dropped in was unsuitable for the conditions as it was not warm enough. The boots they wore soon fell apart in the conditions and a local shoemaker was employed to make new ones.

The first attack was carried out on 30 December 1944, which led to the destruction of three German vehicles. On 1 January1945, an SAS team sent down 34 mortar bombs from 900 feet away on houses occupied by German soldiers and Italian fascist units in the town of Borghetto di Vara. Two lorries were destroyed by a Bren gun as the mortars were fired. This attack led to the withdrawal of the soldiers from the town that evening. On 4 January, a road was mined, destroying a German lorry, killing 12 and injuring eight. Two days later a German staff car was shot up, killing the occupant, a high-ranking Italian fascist. It had also contained an estimated 125 million Italian lire, which would amount to around 54 thousand pounds or around 82 thousand US dollars. On 11 January, a German column was attacked by around 30 of the SAS. They destroyed a captured British staff car and trailer, a German car and trailer, a ten-ton lorry and 23 dead German soldiers. The next day, Italian fascists started to burn houses nearby as reprisal, knowing that the local populous knew what was going on. The SAS retaliated by attacking them with mortars as they went around burning houses. The Italians called in reinforcements, but these were strafed by four American P-47 Thunderbolts that just happened to be in the area. This lucky encounter gave the Germans further impression that a much larger force was operating in the area. Two captured German soldiers said they were part of a force to search and destroy a British force of around 400 paratroopers.

At dawn on 19 January 1945, 2SAS troop moved into their ambush position in an abandoned village carrying two Vickers machine guns. A fast-flowing river flowed through the village and its noise was so great that it drowned all other noise when you got close to it. Once in position, they awaited the Germans who were approaching, and the first noise they heard was the faint but distinctive clatter of horses' hooves. The horses were dragging along artillery in two separate columns followed by German soldiers. The SAS troop waited for the two columns to converge before they began the ambush. The two Vickers guns began to tear apart the Germans, causing them to panic and find any form of cover as the bullets ripped through soldiers, horses and vehicles. Any Germans that tried to escape via the river were picked off with small arms fire. Many soldiers and horses now lay dead as a company of German ski soldiers; some 900 feet away began to converge on the SAS troop. They were spotted moving in on them. The SAS troop had no choice but to withdraw quickly back the way they came when they then saw some more German soldiers climbing the same mountain some 1800 feet in front of them. They needed to avoid ending up in a pincer movement so moved off the track and into the snow, which in places was waist-deep, to ensure they made it to the village before the Germans. They could then get back to their mules and ammunition. After the very arduous climb through deep snow, the SAS troop then had a ten-mile march to Coloretta which, by the end, left the men very exhausted. They made it back to Coloretta at 0700 on 20 January. The raid had initially been borne out of the intelligence that said Mussolini would pass through en route to visit the Monte Rosa Division on the Gothic line.

Below the SAS troop, by about half a mile, were two German companies. SAS commander Walker-Brown had split them into patrols of four and told them to head for a set RV point. As Walker-Brown led his party towards the village of Rio, the Germans opened fire on them, meaning that they needed to push onto Rio as quickly as they could. On reaching Rio, it was not long before German artillery started to rain down on them but they had to continue north towards a rather large mountain called Monte Gottero. The men spent the night at the bottom of the mountain before, at dawn, they began the 4491 ft climb. The climb would be through waist-deep snow, meaning that the leading man was changed every five minutes to reduce fatigue. They made it to the top at 2100, reaching the village of Montegroppo. The men had now been marching for 60 hours and were all shattered, falling asleep within seconds of lying down. Their respite was short-lived; however, as a partisan woke up Walker-Brown after they had been asleep for two hours, warning him that the Germans were only an hour away on foot. Walker-Browned rallied the men and helped pull them to their feet. Sure enough, an hour after the SAS had left, the village was attacked. They carried on walking and by midday had made it to Buzzo and RV with the rest of the SAS. They then set off through the deep snow to hide up in the mountains. Finally, the men could get a good 12 hours of sleep before needing to move again as the Germans approached Buzzo. On 25 January 1945, the Germans sent out some Mongol troops, who had defected to the Germans after harsh treatment and exploitation at the hands of the USSR. Walker-Brown moved his men southeast to the village of Nola, which was deserted, before finally being able to return to their main base at Rossano. The men recuperated for several days, but many were getting sick and on 2 February, 2SAS's medical officer parachuted in to help deal with them. 2SAS continued its attacks during early to mid-February, although they had now lost the element of surprise. The local populous, who had been treated brutally by the Germans for helping the SAS, no longer wanted to support them. By mid-February, Walker-Brown sent through a request that he wanted to exfiltrate 2SAS.

The operation had been successful, with very little cost to 2SAS. The six that were caught by Italian soldiers were kept by the Italians and survived the war in a POW camp. If they had been turned over to the Germans, they would most certainly have been shot. They had killed maybe up to 150 German soldiers, along with 23 enemy vehicles. As the 2SAS withdraw, a German Officer who was having sex with an Italian girl was captured and taken along with them.

As 2SAS left Italy, another 2SAS operation, Operation Cold Comfort, was about to commence with an advanced party dropped into northern Italy. Under the command of Littlejohn, they landed at the DZ (Drop Zone) on 15 February, before the rest of the SAS arrived. They were given away to the Germans almost instantly by a partisan and Littlejohn was captured by mountain troops on 17 February, along with many partisans and the Littlejohn's 2IC (Second in Command). Four B24 Liberator bombers dropped the SAS over the DZ; there should have been six Liberators but two had become separated. Again, some of those dropped had become widely dispersed, with some 25 miles away from the DZ. Operation Cold Comfort had been already in decline. The mission had been to block the main rail lines through the Brenner Pass by causing a landslide, which would have had a dramatic effect on German reinforcements moving south. A month into Cold Comfort, it became apparent that the main objective was impossible to achieve due to the amount of enemy activity. The men spent most of their time in hiding and attempts to supply and reinforce by air were unsuccessful. Littlejohn and Corporal Crowley were captured and then executed under Hitler's Commando Order. Eventually on 31 March 1945, the situation had worsened to the point that the only option was to exfiltrate them.

Chapter Twelve
France 1944

The SRS was now back as 1SAS and before moving into France, they found themselves back in Britain awaiting the invasion of France. Operation Overlord would see the invasion of German-occupied Western Europe by Allied forces. The operation commenced on 6 June 1944 with the Normandy landings (Operation Neptune; more commonly known as D-Day). A 12,000-plane airborne assault preceded an amphibious assault involving almost 7,000 vessels. Nearly 160,000 troops crossed the English Channel on 6 June; more than three million allied troops were in France by the end of August 1944.

The SAS was now under 21st Army group and ordered to remove the familiar beige-coloured beret for a red airborne one that many of the men disliked, especially Mayne, who continued to wear his beige beret. The new chain of command annoyed Bill Stirling greatly. The plan during the invasion of France was for the SAS to parachute in and act as a barrier between the German reserves and the landing beaches. Bill Stirling knew what his brother would have said, as again, the SAS were not being used in the way he had envisaged they should be. With a stern letter from Bill Stirling backed up by his officers, the plan was amended. The SAS would now drop deeper into France in small parties and destroy the Germans lines of communication, whilst arming and training small groups of French Freedom fighters. In Bill Stirling's letter, he had listed several criticisms of the lack of understanding of the SAS's capabilities. He was asked to withdraw these comments, but he refused; not long after, Bill Stirling put his resignation in as the CO of 2SAS. Bill Stirling's 2IC, Brian Franks, became the new CO of 2SAS. The change of command hit morale and a few men wanted to be RTU'd. Franks had an enormous task to get the SAS ready for what would be its biggest role in the war to date. As well as 1 and 2SAS, there were now 3 and 4SAS, as well as a Belgian independent company, and they had collectively become the SAS brigade.

On 1 June 1944, the amended order that Bill Stirling had fought so hard for finally came through. The focus of 1SAS's role would be hundreds of miles south of Normandy. Given the names Operation Bulbasket and Houndsworth, the idea was for them to cut off reinforcements and cause as many supply problems as possible. Bullbasket would see 'B' Squadron establish a base in the Vienne region. 'A' Squadron would be involved in Houndsworth and based at Massif du Morvan. There they would cut and sabotage the railway lines between Lyon and Paris and arm local groups of Freedom Fighters, known as the Maquis.

4SAS was the French regiment and they were to be dropped into Brittany to give the Germans a headache. On 6 June 1944, 36 of them would parachute in and begin training the Maquis to prevent the Germans reinforcing Normandy. The second stage, Operation Cooney, would take place on 7 June and would see the insertion of 18 three- and five-man patrols, whose task was to destroy as many railway links as possible between Brittany and Normandy. On 8 June, the SAS saboteurs from Operation Cooney landed on French soil. Quickly gathering in their parachutes and burying them before regrouping, realised they were five miles away from the intended DZ. They had 48 hours to wreak as much havoc as they could to the railway system. They spent 24 hours trying to find out where they were one of them ended up asking a local at a farm, only to have a German lorry turn up there. Rather than be captured, he killed all seven Germans and then spent the next week hiding; the Germans had instigated a large manhunt. Being a French paratrooper, it was easy for him to get new papers from the French resistance and blend in with the local populous until he could link up with 3SAS.

The secondary mission of Operation Cooney, once they had run out of supplies, was to RV with the rest of 3SAS. 3SAS established two bases: Dingson and Samwest (although Samwest was soon destroyed by the Germans). The survivors of the German attack fled to Dingson Base near the Village of St Marcel, which was not far from the coastal port of Vannes. It wasn't long before the patrol at Dingson met up with the FFI (Forces Françaises de l'Intérieur). They made contact with Colonel Morice, the regional commander. They had impressive capabilities, which led to 3SAS at Dingson requesting more men and supplies to aid the FFI. Colonel Morice had a force of around 2000 that had been brought together in a 500-hectare camp.

The supplies came on 13 June when 25 Stirling Bombers dropped 700 containers and a further eight men. The eight men and the containers had landed slightly off target. Not long after they had landed, they searched for as many supply containers as they could find before finding somewhere to lay up. They found a farmhouse where a woman was living on her own after her husband had been deported to Germany. After feeding the men she hid them in the attic, knowing the Germans would come looking for them. The Germans had been tipped off when some of the containers landed in a chateau that they occupied. They turned up at the cottage the next day, but as they were leaving, one of the soldiers saw some boot prints. This led them to go back and conduct a search of the farmhouse. The first German who tried to make it upstairs was shot dead; the rest withdrew to the front of the house before coming under effective fire from the attic. The SAS threw several grenades, although one detonated in the attic, wounding three and filling the attic with thick acrid smoke that pushed the SAS out. The SAS now had to fight their way out of the farmhouse. The German fire was so intense that it forced them back inside. They continued to fight back until they were running so low on ammunition that they had no choice but to surrender to the Germans. The farmhouse was burnt to the ground and the eight SAS men were all taken as POWs.

By 17 June, Bourgoin had 16 officers and 171 men at the St Marcel base. Operation Cooney had been a success; it had severely disrupted the flow of German reinforcements and forced a division to have to move by road instead of rail. Only a few of the SAS from that operation had not made it to the new camp at St Marcel. On the night of 17 June, General McLeod sent a message to the SAS telling them to continue with the guerrilla-style warfare, avoid large battles and continue arming the FFI. The SAS's luck ran out on 18 June when some German military police strayed too close to the camp in the early hours and an FFI machine gun post opened up on them, killing seven and capturing one. At 8:30am, the Germans launched an attack with around 500 men. They attacked the eastern edge of the camp, which was defended in the main by the SAS. With the attack not making much headway, the Germans called for reinforcements, including fire support in the shape of mortars. The Germans started to move in via the cornfields and came up against the very well-organised SAS defence. As they approached, the Bren Guns opened up on them, cutting them down as if they were walking across no-man's land towards the enemy trenches in World War One.

In the afternoon, the Germans attacked again with a greater force. They gained ground and some strategic points. Despite a well-executed counterattack by the SAS and FFI (French Forces of the Interior) in the evening, it was decided that it would be best to withdraw Bourgoin before the reports of German reinforcements came to fruition. They left via the northern flank during the night as, for some strange reason; the Germans had not covered this. The Germans had lost 300 men during the battle, compared to 6 SAS and 25 FFI. As retribution, the Germans attacked the surrounding villages in a barbaric manner, targeting anyone suspected of being connected in any manner to the FFI. They also began the hunt for the SAS. Some of them were found by a collaborator who led the Germans to them, and they were all shot. This angered Bourgoin, and he sent a message via the FFI to German high command stating that captured German soldiers would also now be shot in a similar fashion. However, this threat fell on deaf ears as a further 16 SAS soldiers were executed over the next few weeks. Many of the men from 4SAS managed to escape into allied controlled areas of France or back to Britain.

Soldiers from 1SAS were dropped into France on 11 June and, as was often the case, ended up a long distance from the intended DZ. Once they had found their location, they were told to wait for 24 hours, and the local Maquis would come and pick them up. They came in a very noisy 45-seater bus. The noise was due to the fact it was running on wood. The process, called wood gasification, works by organic material being converted into a combustible gas under the influence of heat - the process reaches a temperature of 1400°C (2550°F).

It was in the 1920s, that German engineer Georges Imbert developed a wood gas generator for mobile use. The gases were cleaned and dried and then fed into the vehicle's combustion engine, which barely needed to be adapted. The Imbert generator was then mass produced from 1931 onwards and used almost exclusively in Europe.

The SAS soldiers boarded the bus and poked their rifles through the windows once they had been told how to open them. They were to be taken to the Maquis Camille camp. It took a further couple of days for all from 1SAS who had parachuted in to link up. The bus was then used to choose and appropriate DZ for the rest of 1SAS 'A' Squadron. Three planes left Britain with 64 SAS on board. When they got to the DZ, it was heavily shrouded in mist. The planes circled, hoping an opening would appear, but it never did. They had no choice but to return to Britain. One plane carrying 16 men never made it back and no trace of it has ever been found. Four days later, the SAS were able to parachute in with a successful drop. In the days that followed, 'A' Squadron got itself organised, with the Germans totally unaware. The SAS and Maquis mounted their first ambush on a German and White Russian detachment that had been out learning, funnily enough, ambush techniques. The ambush was a resounding success, with 31 German soldier's dead.

The next day, the Germans came back to collect their dead and as they did so, a further 14 German soldiers were killed. This sent the Germans into a rage and meant that the local populous would pay the price. They ravaged two villages, burning them to the ground and killing the odd civilian who had not fled. The next day the Germans, with 250 men, attacked a chateau being used by the Maquis as a hospital. Most of the patients were evacuated to the surrounding forest with the Germans in pursuit, until they came under heavy fire from the Maquis hidden in the trees. This prompted the Germans to mortar the area, with explosions splitting trees in two and sending wood splinters in all directions. The SAS was asked to help with a counterattack and moved up to a road that was the only one leading to the forest. The idea was that as the Germans left, the SAS would attack a short stretch of road. Around 50 Germans moved along the road and were closing in on the SAS. When they were just within a few feet, two Bren guns opened up. Only about ten men escaped uninjured from the ambush.

During the night, the SAS and Marquis moved from their current camp to a new one, knowing that it would only be a matter of time before the Germans attacked their current camp. The next morning, the Germans did indeed find the abandoned camp. Annoyed that they had not captured or killed anyone, they went to the local village, took all the men for interrogation and gang raped a 14-year-old girl. Nineteen men were lined up and executed and the church priest was pushed off the belfry on his church tower with a noose round his neck.

Chapter Thirteen

It was 30 June 1944, Seekings along with his patrol, was laid up, feeling rather wet and cold. They had been in France for 20 days now. They had moved 60 miles through German occupied territory with very little food and water and morale was starting to run low. They still needed to locate the main SAS base and link up. The Germans, fully aware of the SAS presence in France, were doing their very best to hunt them down and kill them. It was a case of moving around regularly to stay one step ahead of the Germans. Another twelve men from 1SAS 'D' Squadron were dropped into France on 4 July to be dropped off at a DZ some 30 miles south of Paris. The SAS was playing a key role in the sabotaging of German supply lines, especially the railways. The DZ however had been revealed after the torture of a Maquis. German Military Police and French Fascist Paramilitaries surrounded the DZ.

As the men dropped to the ground, they were picked up; at the same time, a Bf 110 was trying to shoot at the aircraft dropping the men. It dived into the clouds and managed to get away, safely returning to Britain. All but three of the SAS patrol dropped that night were captured. Those that had not been seriously injured were interrogated and tortured to see if they would give anything up. They were later executed by a firing squad and the two who were too injured to stand in front of a firing squad were given a lethal injection. All of this was undertaken following Hitler's 'Commando Order' issued on 18 October 1942, which said that all enemy commandos captured should be executed. It is widely believed that what happened at Dieppe and on a small raid on the Channel Island of Sark by the Small-Scale Raiding Force brought Hitler's rage to a head and led him to devise and issue the 'Commando Order.'

The SAS were now frequently being dropped into France, only to spend the first few days being spent chased by Germans. On 25 July, the American VII Corps launched their third attempt to break out of the Cotentin Peninsula. The attacked followed a large-scale bombing raid by hundreds of B17 Flying Fortresses.

The offensive was a success and by 8 August, Le Mans was in Allied hands. Mayne had decided to parachute into Morvan to assess future plans as well as help boost morale. He was pleased with how things had gone with Operation Houndsworth. Some of the SAS squadrons now had Jeeps that were dropped in during July. This made for easier travelling and the planning of more audacious raids, including the destruction of a synthetic oil plant. One of the squadrons also now had a six-pounder gun, which was great for destroying convoys of lorries. Two of the fatalities attributed to Operation Houndsworth occurred on 19 July. A patrol of seven departed on 18 July on bicycles to an RV in the Foret de Dames. The following day, four others left, including two 'Originals' from L Detachment, and met up with the other seven. On the morning of 20 July, the Jeep ran into a German convoy and during the brief firefight, two SAS soldiers were killed. The rest of the raid was successful, with a section of railway line destroyed between Entrains and Cosne. The destruction of a section of line led to the derailment of an ammunition train, including the destruction of a couple of Flak guns. During Operation Houndsworth, the Lyon to Paris rail line was blown up 22 times. The squadron captured 132 POWs and killed or wounded 220 Germans. They also identified 30 targets for the Royal Air Force. All for the loss of ten men killed and eight wounded. The operation wound up on 6 September 1944.

On 9 August Mayne drove north and later, on arrival in Touchy, had a brief five-minute chat with his men before shooting off again. Mayne was wanted back in Britain to discuss the next operations, but he wanted some action. He continued his drive north towards Orléans, where 'D' Squadron were. Mayne spoke to the CO and suggested that due to the strong German presence, they should stick to reconnaissance and information-gathering.

The rest of 1SAS 'B' Squadron was parachuted into France on 15 August, initially just an advanced party to start Operation Haggard. Again, they would work with the Maquis. Their orders were to cause 'mayhem' and to choose their own targets. On 21

August, 'B' Squadron took part in its first ambush of Operation Haggard. This entailed ambushing some high-ranking German officers as they returned back to the front after a weekend's R&R. The ambush left 25 Germans dead and the following day, another ambush left 55 dead. The Germans tried to reduce the chances of an ambush by cutting back any foliage 50 feet either side of the Bourges-to-Nerves Road and placing machine gunners on the tops of lorries. Neither technique reduced the impact of ambushes. One ambush on 25 August targeted a column of infantry with horse-drawn artillery that was moving away from Bourges to attack the advancing American forces.

It was a joint ambush with the SAS and Maquis, and they made use of road works on one stretch of road, hiding charges in the rubble, which would be detonated when the convoy was alongside them. Around 500 Germans were killed by the explosion and subsequent firefight, with the SAS suffering a casualty. On the next attack on 27 August, the point of attack was on two bridges on the same road being guarded by SS troops. Alongside 1SAS, some fresh in the field 3SAS French soldiers joined, along with the Maquis. Whilst 1SAS killed the guards and blew the bridges, 3SAS and the Maquis blocked the road. The rest of the SS had by now been alerted to the attack and sent in some stiff resistance, which included 20mm guns mounted on lorries. One 1SAS soldier was killed and one injured; the rest managed to escape, even going unnoticed as they drove coolly past another German convoy. The lorries at the back of the convoy finally realised who they were and started trying to push the various cars off the road, managing to push one car containing Maquis into a ditch. A motorcycle sidecar decided to turn around and give chase but was lost by a car full of 1SAS taking a few sharp turns down various side streets. It was not long after Bourges was liberated and 1SAS felt the full appreciation of the locals. When the Americans turned up expecting to find the Germans, the Germans had already fled and were ten miles down the road.

Operation Haggard was wound up at the beginning of September 1944 after 4SAS overran it with their own much larger operation, 'Operation Spenser'. 4SAS had fanned out across the Loire Valley in squadrons, ambushing the Germans and generally causing mayhem, starting on 29 August, involving 317 men and equipped with 54 jeeps. They destroyed 120 vehicles and captured 2500 prisoners. The idea was to keep biting the retreating German forces and try to keep them off balance. The SS was still finding it difficult, and some had had enough. They were slowly becoming trapped on all sides by the advancing Germans. Bourgoin saw a chance to get them to surrender and sent off a Lieutenant to see if he could negotiate. The Germans seemed more interested in the Jeep than the two men from the SAS. However, knowing that the end was coming, they agreed to surrender rather than fight to the last man and save themselves. Some 3000 Germans surrounded to 4SA; some would only surrender to the Americans out of fear of what the French might do to them. Operation Spenser ended on 14 September and also concluded 4SAS's operations in France. 4SAS had lost 74 men; 25 had been executed by the Germans during their three and a half months of operations. 3SAS had lost 60 months since its first operation in July. Both 3 and 4SAS had at times faced a determined enemy and fought overwhelming odds with bravery and heroism.

Chapter Fourteen

1SAS, due to the heavy German presence, had ended up doing more reconnaissance work in France. After Mayne, had left on 9 August 1944, 1SAS were busy finding suitable DZ for an advanced party for Operation Kipling and building fuel dumps for the advancing Americans. Operation Kipling was the name of the next operation 1SAS 'C' Squadron would be involved with. The 'C' Squadron advanced party dropped into France in the early hours of 14 August, followed four days later by a further 13 men from 'C' Squadron. 'C' Squadron was then tasked with finding suitable landing sites for gliders to bring in the rest of 'C' Squadron, although that plan was changed so that the rest of 'C' Squadron would land in DC-3s at Rennes airfield and then drive to the now established 'C' Squadron base in Jeeps. With the whole of 'C' Squadron in France, they began reconnaissance patrols. Some of the patrols were called 'road watch,' as that was exactly what they were doing - watching a particular road and counting the number of vehicles moving along it. In many ways, these patrols were much safer than ambushing or attacking the Germans. The chance of being spotted or detected in the various OPs (Observation Posts) was very slim. However, on 23 August, they had taken a Jeep out to go and find a garage that could repair a broken weld on the Vickers machine mounting. They arrived in Les Ormes just as an SS unit was about to execute 25 civilians. The first Jeep opened up, taking the SS by surprise. The SS returned very accurate fire, shooting one SAS soldier, Harrison, through the hand and a killing the other, Hall, who was in the Jeep. The second Jeep joined in the fight and gave the civilians time to escape. They left Hall and got Harrison to jump in, before leaving Les Ormes and the civilians to fend for themselves, minus a few Germans who now lay dead. Two SAS soldiers returned later for Hall's body, to find that he had already been placed in a coffin by the villagers, who said they would bury him. The SS were still close by so care had to be taken in attending the funeral a couple of days later.

1SAS 'A' Squadron returned home on 8 September after just over three months in France, whilst 'C' Squadron continued with Operation Kipling. It was towards the end of September that a communist group of Maquis offered to pay 30,000 francs for a Bren gun. This was accepted and the money changed hands, making 'C' Squadron quite rich.

So far, 2SAS had heard little about what 1SAS were up to. They had spent their time in initially in Scotland, partly due to having a new CO called Franks and 140 new recruits to train. They moved down to Salisbury Plains in June, waiting to be sent to France. Their first operation was Operation Defoe, which would see 21 men dropped into France on 19 July to perform reconnaissance patrols to aid the British Second Army in Normandy. The reports they sent out seemed to be of no real interest to the British or the Americans and the Operation ended on 23 August. On 3 August, another 59 men were dropped into France as part of Operation Dunhill. The five patrols were to disrupt German activity in advance of Operation Cobra, which was the name of the American breakout from Normandy. The breakout moved much quicker than planned and four of the patrols were relieved within 24 hours.

The fifth patrol managed to send back intelligence on German movements. Their more interesting task came up when they were approached by an MI9 agent. MI9 was tasked during the war with aiding resistance fighters in enemy-occupied territory and recovering Allied troops who found themselves behind enemy lines. The MI9 agent asked the SAS if they could assist with 150 Allied airmen who were currently hidden in a forest inside German lines some 50 miles away. These airmen had been collected as part of Operation Sherwood and had been smuggled into a central position by agents awaiting the arrival of Allied forces. The MI9 agent had not been able to move them due to the Americans refusing to lend the agent any suitable transport. The SAS helped themselves to four buses and six cars and drove them through what was left of the German lines, who seemed to just run away or lose the will to fight. The Americans proved to be a bit of a handful as all were quite drunk; the British aircrew meanwhile had a command structure and were not a problem. All the aircrew were taken to Le Mans and handed over.

With Operation Dunhill completed, 2SAS returned to Britain, ready for their next operation, Operation Trueform. This operation had not been thought through and put together at speed due to how fluid things were in France. It would last for a maximum of three weeks and 101 men from 2SAS, along with the Belgium SAS detachment, would destroy German road and rail transport between Rouen and Paris. The main problem was that there was no accurate information, and the movement and fluidity were changing at a rapid pace. The operation had limited success for five days until the SAS linked up with them.

Operation Rupert was to sabotage railway lines between Nancy and Châlons-Sur-Marne. An advanced party sent over, but sadly the Stirling bomber carrying them crashed into a hillside near to the DZ, killing everyone except one SAS soldier. A second advanced party was successfully dropped two weeks later. It was not until the end of August that Operation Rupert had all the required men in France. Other than the odd skirmish, the Germans were retreating at quite a fast pace to the east and the Vosges mountains. When the Americans linked up with 2SAS, they initially got them to undertake reconnaissance missions until Patton, who did not like the British, had them escorted away from the 3rd Army. Operation Loyton was another operation to cause havoc to the Germans.

The SAS advance party, led by Captain Duce, parachuted into the Vosges on 12 August 1944. The drop zone was in a deeply wooded, mountainous area 40 miles west of Strasbourg. As they landed, the Maquis decided to take all the containers as payment for the SAS landing in their field. The advance party would not carry out any action, but simply find suitable targets and a DZ for the rest of 2SAS involved in the operation. As they began reconnaissance patrols, they soon realised that there were more than 5000 Germans in the area, who seemed to be the arrowhead for a much larger force. The main party, commanded by Lieutenant Colonel Franks, dropped into France on 30 August 1944. Their landing was not without incident, when a container filled with ammunition exploded on contact with the ground. A slightly funny and tragic incident befell a member of the Maquis; he was helping move the containers but killed himself by eating a plastic explosive that he thought was a kind of cheese. The following day, after landing in France, the SAS started patrolling and set up observation posts. Almost immediately they became aware that their presence had been betrayed to the Germans. The SAS, due to the number of attacks and ambushes, led the Germans to believe that a far larger force was operating in the area. The operation was going so well that on 19 and 20 September, reinforcements were parachuted in, which consisted of another twenty men and six Jeeps. The Jeeps gave 2SAS greater freedom of movement and the ability to change their tactics. The Jeeps were used to patrol roads and shoot up German road convoys and staff cars. One patrol found an SS unit as it assembled. The patrol drove through the town and opened up on the SS, killing many of them.

The Germans tried to locate the SAS base but knew that the local populous would be assisting them. To try to gain intelligence, they rounded up all the male residents of Moussey between the ages of 16 and 60 and arrested them. After being interrogated, they were transported to concentration camps, from which only 70 returned after the war. Two German agents tried to infiltrate by masquerading as French agents, but one of the Maquis with the SAS had seen one of them with Germans and they were quickly disposed of by the French.

By the start of October, with Patton's army stalled due to a stretched supply line that was unable to get supplies to the American Army, the likelihood that the Americans would be able to relieve the SAS had dwindled. The operation was ended after three months, even though the original intention had only been for a two-week operation. Members of 2SAS spilt up into smaller groups to make it harder for them to be detected as they made their way back. thirty had been executed by the SD (Sicherheitsdienst), the intelligence agency of the SS, some of them executed at the Natzweiler-Struthof concentration camp in the Vosges Mountains. During its time in France, it was estimated that the SAS had killed or wounded 7753 enemy soldiers and personnel, captured 4764, destroyed 29 locomotives, 348 lorries and 141 cars, and one German bomber was shot down amazingly by a single Bren gun.

Chapter Fifteen
The Final Push 1945

On Boxing Day 1944, 2SAS were put on 24 hours' notice to be ready to parachute into the Ardennes in Belgium. To hunt down small groups of Germans who were dressed in American uniforms and able to speak fluent English with an American accent. These groups were causing a real headache for the Americans. The Belgian detachment of the SAS was already there and had been operating in France and Belgium since the end of July 1944. During the first few weeks, they had attacked the German 15th Army as it retreated from the advancing American 3rd Army, with Montgomery's failed attempt to capture the Rhine with Operation Market Garden and the stretched supply lines that Patton had faced bringing his move forward to a halt. This resulted in static warfare not too dissimilar to that found in World War 1, but without the network of trenches. In some places the Germans put up stiff resistance; the Scheldt Estuary was one, and it took the Allied soldiers some six weeks of bloody fighting to get rid of the Germans. Once the Germans were gone, the estuary still needed clearing of any mines before any ships could enter Antwerp some 85 days after its capture. It had proved a real headache for Montgomery and slowed the pace of the advance right down, losing speed and the element of surprise. It also gave Hitler a false sense of security that Germany was not defeated, and he began planning an offensive in the Ardennes with the aim of retaking Antwerp. The German advance was halted on 26 December 1944, just outside Dinant.

The Belgian SAS had arrived in the Ardennes a couple of days before Christmas 1944 and immediately started to conduct reconnaissance patrols. As the Germans were pushed back, the Belgian SAS came under the command of the 6th Airborne division whilst conducting operations around the villages of Wellin and Bure. Two hundred French soldiers from 4SAS arrived on Christmas Eve 1944 to protect the left flank of the advancing Americans. The weather in the area was cold and harsh, reaching -20°C. Laying up and waiting to conduct an ambush left many freezing, almost to the point of hypothermia.

1SAS was back in Britain in September 1944, with Mayne working out where they could next be best utilised after the conclusion of Operation Haggard. In October 1944, 1SAS moved itself out to Belgium as it was felt that was where they were likely be most needed in Europe. In the run-up to Christmas, the various Squadrons were assigned different roles. 'B' Squadron carried out reconnaissance patrols and 'C' Squadron attacked the Wessem and Noorer canals.

The German counteroffensive in the Ardennes on 16 December 1944 took the Allies by surprise. As the size of the offensive became known, the SAS was quickly redeployed. The German offensive was supported by several smaller operations called Bodenplatte, Unternehmen, Währung, and Greif. Germany's aim was to split the American and British Allied line in half, before recapturing Antwerp and then proceeding to surround and destroy the four Allied armies. This was in the hope that it would force the Western Allies to have to negotiate a peace treaty that would end up in the Axis's favour. With this treaty in place, Hitler then wanted to turn his full attention to the East. The 'Battle of the Bulge,' as it became known, was planned under the utmost secrecy, ensuring only the minimal of radio traffic and moving soldiers and equipment under the cover of darkness. Although the Third U.S. Army's intelligence staff predicted a major German offensive, it still caught the Allies by surprise.

The Allies were preoccupied with their own offensive, had become a little too confident and made too little use of aerial reconnaissance. The final blow that got the offensive underway was the near-complete surprise against a weakly defended section of the Allied line. The Germans made use of the overcast weather to ensure that the now numerically superior Allied air forces would be grounded. Fierce resistance from Allied forces on the northern shoulder of the offensive around Hofen and Elsenborn, and in the south around Bastogne, blocked German access to key roads that they needed if they were to ensure success. This, along with terrain that favoured the Allies, meant the German timetable started to lag behind schedule. Allied reinforcements, including Patton's Third Army, along with improving weather conditions, meant that Allied aircraft could take to the sky and the offensive was soon halted. The Germans lost many men. For the Americans, it was the bloodiest battle they had fought so far. They had 19,246 men killed and 62,489 wounded, while the British had 200 men killed and 969 wounded. A total of 26,851 Allied soldiers were either captured or missing. The German losses were even heavier, with an estimated 84,834 killed, wounded, or captured, although other estimates have this number as high as 100,000 and as low as 60,000.

1SAS tasked with a range of activities, from killing parachute troops as they landed or hunting them down, to preventing Germans dressed in American uniforms from crossing a bridge by blowing it up.

3 and 4SAS returned from the Ardennes to Britain in February 1945, before moving on 3 April to Mushroom Farm transit camp in Essex. Not long after, they were told that they were going to be dropped en-mass into northeast Holland in advance of the First Canadian Army. Their objective was to seize and then hold key road and rail bridges, eighteen in total, as part of Operation Amherst. The Canadians would then link up with the SAS 48 hours later. On 7 April, 684 French SAS climbed aboard 47 Stirling. One team was led by a French 3SAS lieutenant, Duno. His team leapt into the cold night sky, landing only one mile away from the actual DZ. Duno's objective was the Appelscha bridge, which he captured by 6am on 8 April. They then spent the day looking for any stranded SAS but finding no more. The next day they attacked a German staff car, dragging out the German officer and handing him into the Dutch. In only a few days, Duno had some 40 German prisoners and had commandeered a farm and used the empty pigsties, since the Germans had taken all the pigs to house the POWs.

Another team, led by Boutinot, had landed east of Assen, near to a small village called Gasselte. Four teams of ten had landed close together so they joined up to form one larger unit. Their first ambush was on a German Red Cross lorry, shooting it up and capturing the German doctor, who spoke very good French, and making use of him. Later that day, an attack was mounted against the Gasselte headquarters of the Dutch Fascists, finding some Dutch SS hiding within the village. The 3SAS showed no mercy, slitting throats and dragging them behind Jeeps after they decided to ignore the Genève convention. This was simply due to the atrocities the Germans had undertaken not just in Holland, but also in France, including the execution of any captured SAS soldier. Based in and around Groningen was the SS Dutch Brigade, which was now cornered by the advancing Allies and the North Sea so had nowhere to withdraw. They made a stand, fighting very impressively.

The Belgian SAS detachment reached Coverdon in Holland on 7 April 36 hours after Canadian forces had liberated it. On 8 April, the Belgian SAS became attached to the 1st Polish armoured division to act as their eyes and ears. On 9 April, the SAS and 1st Polish made their way north towards Groningen and towards the North Sea to cut off the SS soldiers withdrawing away from the advancing 3SAS. The Belgian SAS soldiers made good progress. They had realised that the Jeep had certain weaknesses; it had the advantage of speed but weak firepower and lack of armour. To counter this, the Belgian SAS carried ten men in a lorry alongside the Jeep, acting as infantry. This tactic got them to the southern side of the Mussel canal just before midday on 12 April without a casualty. They were only 20 miles from the coast, but the Dutch had told them a large force of German Kreigsmarine were dug in at the village of Veele.

The two squadrons of SAS, 'A' and 'B' Squadron, split up along the canal banks of Veele, going in opposite directions. 'A' Squadron lost a man when he was shot by a sniper as they headed along the canal. 'A' Squadron was trying to figure out how they were going to get across when a boat was noticed on the other side. Two men, Bastin and Segelaar, tried to pull it back across whilst the Jeeps with 'A' Squadron laid down some heavy covering fire. The Germans finally decided to retaliate with their own intense barrage of small arms fire and mortars. The mortars shattered the trees surrounding 'A' Squadron. 'B' Squadron was now coming under effective German fire as they tried to find a way across the canal. Their only choice was to run along some lock gates and leave the Jeeps behind. 'A' and 'B' Squadrons fought through and linked up on the northern side of the canal. They could now start clearing the Germans from the village. Any captured Germans were killed, not just, because they were the much-hated SS but due to the fact that any captured German would require precious men being taken away from the fire fight to guard them. The 1st Polish armoured division arrived on 13 April with their Sherman tanks following the Belgian SAS.

By 15 April, the Belgian SAS were in Winschoten, the last town before the sea. The air was filled with the characteristic smell of the seaside.

A German Fort lay on the coast and contained what were now stranded Germans, although they were still ready and happy to fight. The Polish CO wanted the SAS to attack the Fort in daylight across open ground that offered no protection. The Belgian SAS refused unless the Polish would join them in the attack as well. The Polish refused.

Chapter Sixteen

1 and 2SAS were lined up for a joint operation, called Operation Archway. This was the codename for one of the largest and most diverse operations carried out by the Special Air Service during the Second World War. Operation Archway would last between March-May 1945. It was initially intended to support Operation Plunder and Operation Varsity, the crossings of the River Rhine at Rees, Wesel, and south of the Lippe River in North Rhine-Westphalia in Germany by the British Second Army, under Lieutenant-General Dempsey. It went on to support the three British Armoured Divisions in their advance into Germany until the end of the war. The Archway force was under command of Lieutenant Franks and comprised two squadrons, one each from 1 and 2SAS. The idea of Operation Archway was to support the 21st Army Group during Operation Varsity as they made parachute landings across the River Rhine. This was to be the final major airborne operation of the war. The SAS was equipped with an upgraded Jeep which had an armoured windscreen and armour at the front. A .5 Browning machine gun had been added, along with a dozen drums of spare ammunition that were attached to the bonnet and sides of the Jeep. All Jeeps now carried a Bazooka and a Bren gun and had a smoke screen device fitted on the rear. 1 and 2SAS would have 75 of these for the operation. Along with the Jeeps, they had the support of 300 tanks. They were supported by a number of 15-cwt and 3-ton and some of the SAS teams, who were equipped with 3-inch Mortars.

At 1130 on 25 March 1945, Frankforce began crossing the Rhine in amphibious landing craft called the Buffalo. The Buffalo was an amphibious tracked vehicle that had a large open tub at the rear and a ramp for soldiers to disembark. The American Army still has Buffaloes in service in the war in Afghanistan, although these are no relation to the WWII Buffaloes as they are six-wheeled non-amphibious vehicles used to clear mines. The Buffaloes could carry two Jeeps at a time as they shuffled backwards and forwards. On 26 March Frankforce split, with 1SAS conducting reconnaissance patrols for the British 6th Airborne and 2SAS, consisting of 129 soldiers, attached to the 6th Independent Armoured brigade.

1SAS made their first contact with the Germans on 27 March after the Canadian Paratroopers had requested support. 1SAS and its Jeeps moved in across some dead ground towards the German positions. The Germans open fired on one Jeep, revealing the position of a machine gun nest and allowing other Jeeps to move round on its right flank and destroy the position. They continued to attack the German positions, destroying many before the Germans began to withdraw. 1SAS spent the night at a farmhouse before moving out. They had just passed through the village of Ostrich on what seemed like a quiet country road when a German stood up and fired a Panzerfaust, a German anti-tank weapon, at the leading Jeep. This was followed by heavy gunfire. One SAS soldier was shot through the throat and died instantly. The Jeeps tried to reverse back down the road; one accelerated forward, racking a barn with fire from the Vickers machine gun. Three-inch mortars were set up and began raining fire down on the woods; another part of the SAS went to the barn and discovered the Germans hiding out in there. The British paratroopers soon joined the SAS, helping clear the woods of the remaining Germans. In the end, 80 Germans lay dead and 70 were captured. The SAS had two dead and several wounded; one had his arm riddled with bullets; another had a gaping hole in his armpit after a bullet had exploded in it. The wounded were taken back to the British paratrooper lines, while the rest of 1SAS moved on towards Rhade. Once at Rhade, the SAS was asked to hold the town whilst the British Paratroopers took up defensive positions on the railway line to the east. On 28 March 1SAS, was ordered to move back from Rhade and allow the advancing Allied armour to enter.

2SAS joined the 6th Independent Guards near Schermbeck some 13 miles west of the Rhine. As they approached the town of Dulmen on 29 March, they headed along some very muddy roads and tracks, causing one of the Jeeps to become bogged down. As the SAS soldiers tried to free the Jeep, they noticed some Germans a couple of fields away. They were ordered to leave the Jeep and attack them. A couple of them went via the right flank while the others went for a full-frontal attack. It was not long before the Germans were laying down fire at quite a pace. The SAS men pushed forward, one receiving a bullet in the arm, and destroyed the position very efficiently with a grenade, before going back and getting the Jeep unstuck and moving on.

Early in the evening on 7 April, 1SAS were at Petershagen waiting to ford the Weser River. The commandos who had crossed earlier had ended up clashing with the Waffen SS. As the SAS waited to cross, they received sporadic German shelling. They all made it across the river without any casualties to spend the night in a village called Windheim. In the morning, 'D' Squadron made off northeast towards Neustadt. 'A' Squadron acted as their flank protection whilst 'D' Squadron overpowered a small but determined group of SS soldiers. A troop from 'A' Squadron with nine Jeeps headed towards the village of Scheernen. As they moved out of Scheemen, a Dingo Scout car was waiting for them and joined the convoy, shortly before another two Dingo scout cars joined them on the rear. A Panzerfaust was fired at a Dingo and alerted them to a German position in the woods to their left. The SAS dismounted and headed off. As they did so, one of the SAS's Jeeps was knocked out at point blank range by a Panzerfaust, nearly decapitating one SAS soldier who was sitting in the Jeep at the time. Another German soldier was about to fire a Panzerfaust when he was hit by a hail of bullets from a Vickers machine gun and the Panzerfaust exploded, blowing him to bits. The fierce fire fight lasted for some time before the Germans were defeated.

With the Germans defeated, the remaining Jeeps and Dingos went back to the crossroads at which they had first met up. Amazingly, only one Jeep had been lost; they were met by two more SAS Jeeps, one containing Lieutenant McNaught and another with Poat inside. As they debriefed from the last ambush, Seekings noticed that less than 200 feet away, the Germans were moving up from some woods in the east. A mortar was quickly set up and sent six rounds onto their position. In the distance the sound of armoured vehicles could be heard, which everyone assumed meant that the 6th Airborne were catching up. As a further two SAS Jeeps were followed by British armoured cars not far in front. As the Jeeps grew closer, it became evident that they were being fired upon by some German armoured vehicles much further behind them who scored a direct hit with a 30mm cannon shell, causing a Jeep to burst into flames. The four SAS soldiers managed to escape unscathed before one of them was killed by another 20mm round. The SAS was rapidly becoming surrounded by German soldiers as more advanced towards them. At the crossroads, the SAS was fighting off an attack from the east. The Jeeps and their position gave the SAS a good commanding ground in which to be able to lay down some very effective and destructive fire; the British Dingo armoured cars managed to destroy one of the German armoured cars. The Germans continued to diverge and there was no choice but for the SAS to retreat down the road on which they had just been ambushed. By the time, they had all fled, the Germans were within 50 feet of the crossroad. Each Jeep sped off at its top speed of 50mph under a hail of enemy fire. They raced back to friendly lines and requested that tanks go in and clear the woods. Later the SAS went in and recovered two bodies; two other SAS soldiers were still missing. One SAS soldier, Davis, was later found in a hospital morgue in Nienburg after 2SAS had advanced there on 10 April. The other missing SAS soldier, Ferguson, was found dead in another hospital, having been taken in fatally wounded.

Chapter Seventeen

2SAS were in Germany and left Nienburg before continuing east, reaching Esperke on 11 April 1945. They lay up there while armour made its way towards the town of Celle. Celle is a town and capital of the district of Celle, in Lower Saxony, Germany. The town is situated on the banks of the River Aller. Celle was an important garrison location. Elements of the 17th and 73rd Infantry Regiments and the 19th Artillery Regiment were garrisoned in the town. Celle was also the headquarters of a military district command and a military records office.

2SAS made it to Celle at 0500 on 12 April. A local civilian approached 2SAS and told them about the town's concentration camp, which had some severe casualties in need of medical attention. The Celle concentration camp was an annexe of the infamous Belsen concentration camp a few miles to the north. 2SAS went on to investigate the camp and found a high wire fence that had a screen of matting which ensured no one could see what was going on inside. The sentry on duty was ordered to open the gate and what the men saw was truly horrific; there were corpses strewn about and the prisoners so thin they looked like walking skeletons. Some prisoners were barely alive, half covered in manure. The stench of rotting human flesh of both the living and the dead, along with the manure, was so strong your nose could barely deal with it, and it caused almost instant wrenching. 2SAS did what they could and shot a few of the German guard's dead in anger, before requesting that the occupants of Celle, came and looked at what had been going on. They also needed help with the emaciated survivors who only very loosely resembled anything human. 2SAS also sent a message back to brigade to say they had found a concentration camp, which had to be seen to be believed.

On 15 April 1945, a patrol from 1SAS was driving along a sandy track in a dense pine forest when they noticed some men in strange orange and brown uniforms. The men were Hungarian and were there to prevent anyone from leaving after typhoid had broken out in a local prison camp. The SAS continued onward to a crossroad in the forest, when an almost overpowering stench hit them. They turned and made their way down the road to the camp, hoping there may be some British POWs. The road to the camp was pristine and well looked after. What they had found was Belson concentration camp, which put Celle in the shade. The same awful stench hit them along with a similar scene of severely emaciated human beings wandering around, searching for food. They found a huge pit that was full to the brim with naked bodies, simply left there to rot. 1SAS was left just as speechless and numb as 2SAS had been at Celle. There were around 53,000 prisoners, half of them seriously ill and starving. Another 13,000 corpses lay strewn all over the place. There was not much 1SAS could do except go and get help. They had neither the means nor the transport with which to help the vast number in need of medical aid. The 63rd Anti-Tank Regiment, part of 11th Armoured Division, came to do a handover with the SAS. Not much later, Richard Dimbleby sent BBC News the following report:

Here, over an acre of ground, lay dead and dying people. You could not see which was which... The living lay with their heads against the corpses and around them moved the awful, ghostly procession of emaciated, aimless people, with nothing to do and with no hope of life, unable to move out of your way, unable to look at the terrible sights around them ... Babies had been born here, tiny wizened things that could not live ... A mother, driven mad, screamed at a British sentry to give her milk for her child, and thrust the tiny mite into his arms, then ran off, crying terribly. He opened the bundle and found the baby had been dead for days. This day at Belsen was the most horrible of my life.

Later, 1SAS were fumigated due to the fear of lice and other bugs with which many of the prisoners in Belson were infested. Some of the German locals were taken to see Belson for themselves, to truly understand what their fellow countrymen had done. The smell would not leave the SAS men's noses for days; it was like nothing they had ever smelt before or would ever smell again.

After Celle, 2SAS moved quickly towards the River Elbe along with a reconnaissance unit from the 15th division. On 19 April, they entered Neetze, five miles west of Elbe and just 65 miles from Berlin, when they were ordered to halt. 1SAS entered Lüneburg the same day behind tanks dealing with some minor pockets of resistance. Both 1 and 2SAS waited for a week whilst Montgomery planned how his forces would cross the river. Once across, Eisenhower wanted Montgomery to advance to the Baltic and cut off Schleswig-Holstein and Denmark, before proceeding through to seize Kiel Canal. The crossing of the River Elbe would require a large amount of bridging. As well as this, Montgomery estimated that there were eight or nine battalions on the east bank of the Elbe. 1 and 2SAS were joined by the SAS who had taken part in Operation Keystone during early April. Operation Keystone consisted of several Jeep-mounted and airborne teams that had operated south of Ijsselmeer, a shallow artificial lake of 680 square miles in central Holland. Bad weather meant that in the end, the operation was called off, although a column of ten Jeeps headed north from Arnhem to see if they could penetrate German lines. They managed one successful ambush on 18 April when they ambushed marching German soldiers from a wood. The ambush killed 20 soldiers and took another 16 as prisoners. After the ambush, they headed east towards Elbe and the rest of 'Frankforce'.

The crossing of the Elbe occurred on 29 April; 2SAS went across at 3pm. The opposition was generally light with some minor shelling and a few strafing attacks by the German Luftwaffe in the form of the Me-262 twin engine jet fighter, with its powerful cannon and a top speed of over 500mph. The Allied forces captured 1300 German soldiers, before continuing their advance. On 3 May, with 2SAS not far behind, 1SAS headed towards Hamburg, still encountering the odd pockets of resistance.

Chapter Eighteen

On 8 April 1945, Mayne was briefing his men not far from Meppen, Germany. The operation, called Operation Howard, was a mission acting as reconnaissance for the 4th Canadian Armoured Division. The SAS was to be part of the push into northern Germany towards the city of Oldenburg. There was a feeling though that the 2nd Army did not really know how to best utilise the SAS. On 9 April, two columns consisting of 'B' and 'C' squadron set off a few miles apart. The two columns crossed the River Hase in Germany and headed north towards a village called Borger. A Jeep from 'C' Squadron had run into an ambush and lost an officer almost instantaneously when he was shot through the head by a sniper. The rest had jumped out of the Jeep and were crawling along a ditch, trying to head back to the rest of the squadron. Mayne was now racing down the same road and in sight of the men in the ditch. He shouted at them as he raced past, saying that he would pick them up on his way back. As he drove past the woods, one of the SAS soldiers in his Jeep fired with the Vickers guns, and then turned around for a second pass, before pulling the men in the ditch onto the Jeep and racing back down the road to the rest of the column.

By the next day, Operation Howard had made timely progress, with the loss of just one officer. After passing another village called Esterwegen, they ran into an area of woodland that was flooded. The soldiers taking pot shots at them seemed to be getting younger and younger, with some bursting out crying the minute they came under attack. The opposition was getting fiercer though, as German soldiers fought for their homeland. Snipers lay waiting at random points and shots were being fired from the most innocuous places. The SAS treated the Germans with hatred; in North Africa, they had done everything by the book. However, after what had happened to fellow SAS men and the atrocities they had seen, many German POWs were killed or tortured. The SAS though, where possible, did try to abide by the Geneva Convention as they did not want to end up at the same level as the Germans.

By the afternoon of 11 April, 'B' and 'C' squadron had reached the outskirts of Friesoythe, 35 miles to the west of Bremem. As 'B' squadron approached the town, they saw a German lorry; as they got closer, the odd SAS soldier began to wonder if it was a trap. The lorry was now 90 feet in front of the lead SAS Jeep. As they drew closer, the Jeep's machine guns opened up on the lorry. As soon as the guns opened up, mortar fire began to rain down on them. The Jeeps quickly spun round and raced back the way they had come. A direct hit was scored on one Jeep as it leapt into the air with a big yellow and orange flash. The front of the Jeep had vanished and one of its occupants ended up in a ditch of muddy water, still alive and unscathed if rather dirty. Other occupants had also landed in the ditch and emerged wet and dazed a short while later. The mortar bombs continued to rain down as the Jeeps fled the area; the SAS was returning fire. The area was too well defended to approach by road, which was full of snipers and soldiers. One group of SAS managed to get captured after seeing a convoy of lorries and not realising they were German. Once captured, they were taken back to the town. At the same time, Mayne attacked the convoy via his Jeep, but the SAS had no choice but to pull back. They had now lost six Jeeps, four of which were captured by the Germans and the other two destroyed during the battle. All the SAS could do was wait out for the 4th Armoured division to catch up and offer some much needed armour and fire support.

Youngman was one of the ten SAS soldiers captured by the Germans and was handed over to the SS to be tortured for information. The captured men could hear the battle raging on to the west of them. The next morning, the captured SAS men were marched deeper into Germany, away from the advancing Allied forces. As they were paraded through villages, locals would come out and kick and punch them. Many Germans had no idea what had really gone on in their country and the atrocities the Nazi forces had committed. They were marched for several days and arrived at Stalag Xb in Sandbostel on 16 April. The prison was mainly populated with French prisoners, along with some downed aircrew. After a couple of days' respite, the Gestope turned up and tried to gather further intelligence. As they made threats to kill, two of the ten men thought they may as well be killed trying to escape than just be killed. The other eight decided they would take their chances in the prison and that it would not be long before the advancing Allied forces would catch up with them.

The French gave Youngman and the other SAS soldier who wanted to escape a weekly pass, which allowed them to go outside the camp one day a week. The two SAS men strolled out of the entrance, flashing their passes, and made their way west along a main road before diverting down a country lane. By this time, two German tanks had spotted them and had its guns trained on them. The tank commander popped out the top and asked what they were doing. Youngman explained that they had a day pass and were visiting friends. The German OK'd this, told them that they were heading in the wrong direction and sent them on their way. Youngman and the other SAS finally found the Allied line on 25 April, when they came across the Guards Armoured Brigade having breakfast after the smell of fried eggs and bacon had hit their noses. The two men were debriefed and the information they now had on the location of German troops was invaluable. They were then returned to Mayne to make good use of their intelligence.

The Germans were fighting bloodier and bloodier battles as they became more desperate to protect Germany. It had turned into a slogging match between the Allied forces and German forces. On 14 April, a convoy of Jeeps pulled into the side of the road to have a cup of tea. One of the men noticed a small mound in the middle of the road and yelled "STOP!" to the Jeep that was still moving forward, but it was too late and the mine exploded underneath it. One of the men was killed instantaneously and the other two were pulled seriously injured from the twisted wreckage in a scene reminiscent of an IED (Improvised Explosive Device) exploding underneath a Land Rover in Iraq or the early parts of the Afghan war.

As the SAS pushed forward, the conditions became too boggy for the Jeeps and they had to move as tank-borne infantry. By the end of April, nearly all the fighting was over for Mayne and his men. There was still the very odd pocket of resistance from those Germans prepared to die for their country. On 3 May, 2SAS were ordered to accompany the 11th Armoured division to Kiel, encountering the odd stubborn SS patrol. The fighting went on right up to the ceasefire on 5 May 1945. 'Frankforce' began to withdraw through Hamburg on 7 May (VE day), heading back to an RV at Poperinghe in Belgium. As they drove back towards Belgium, they saw huge lines of defeated German soldiers. They began to arrive in Poperinghe on 9 May.

On 10 May, the Belgian SAS was asked to become the first Allied soldiers to enter Flensburg in Germany, not far from the border with Denmark. They had been sent there to stop the Germans crossing the border and help arrest Nazis. They arrested 60 German officers and another 500 soldiers handed themselves over. A notorious Danish collaborator was also caught. The Belgian SAS continued into June, arresting Nazis.

1 and 2SAS were given a similar task from 12 May when they landed in Stavanger, Norway. The Germans had been tasked with dismantling defences and minefields along the coast. The SAS was to continue its search for Nazis. The SAS's time was drawing to a close and Mayne knew this when he returned to Britain in August. Japan had surrendered so there was no need for the SAS in the Far East, although the now released David Stirling had fully intended to get the SAS out there.

On 21 September, the Belgian SAS Squadrons were incorporated into their own army; the French 3 and 4SAS left the Brigade on 1 October. On 8 October 1945, the SAS paraded for the last time before being disbanded on 30 September 1946, closing the first chapter of the SAS. They had fought with valour and learnt many tactics that are still being used today. 'The Originals' had made their mark in history, and Sir David Stirling will always be known for his 'Stirling Work' as the founder of what is possibly the world's most famous military unit.

"Everything we did from start to end contributed to it. Very often, you get to the point where you think, 'Is there any point in carrying on?"

David Stirling

On 30 June 1984 at the opening of the new SAS HQ in Hereford called Stirling Lines. David Stirling stated in his opening speech:

"I have always felt uneasy in being known as the founder of the Regiment. To ease my conscience I would like it to be recognized that I have five co-founders: Jock Lewes and 'Paddy' Blair Mayne of the original 'L' Detachment, SAS; Georges Bergé, whose unit of the Free French joined the SAS in June 1942; Brian Franks, who re-established 21 SAS Regiment after the SAS had been disbanded at the end of the Second World War; and John Woodhouse who created the modern 22 SAS Regiment during the Malayan campaign by restoring the Regiment to its original philosophy."

Sir David Stirling passed away on 4 November 1990 at the age of 74

Glossary

Airspeed Horsa - The Airspeed AS.51 Horsa was a British World War II troop-carrying glider built by Airspeed Limited and subcontractors and used for air assault by British and Allied armed forces. It could carry 25 passengers and 2 crew or equivalent weight of cargo including small vehicles. It was named after Horsa, the legendary 5th century conqueror of southern Britain.

B17 Flying Fortress – The B17 was a four-engine bomber, powered by four Wright R-1820-97 Cyclone turbo and supercharged radial engines developing 1,200 HP. It made its first flight on 28 July 1935 and entered service in 1938. The first B-17s saw combat in 1941, when the British Royal Air Force took delivery of several B-17s for high-altitude missions. As World War II intensified, the bombers needed additional armament and armour. The B-17E, the first mass-produced model Flying Fortress, carried nine machine guns and a 4,000-pound bomb load. It was several tons heavier than the prototypes and bristled with armament.

Bazooka – The Bazooka is a man-portable recoilless rocket antitank weapon, mainly used by the US Army. Also referred to as the "Stovepipe", the bazooka was amongst the first-generation of rocket propelled anti-tank weapons used in infantry combat. In World War Two the M1 and starting with the invasion of Sicily the M1A1. Both had a range of 400 feet and an effective range of 150 feet.

Bombay - The Bristol Bombay was a British troop transport aircraft adaptable for use as a medium bomber flown by the RAF during the Second World War. Its first flight was in June 1935 and the aircraft was retired in 1944. The Bristol Bombay was built to Air Ministry Specification C.26/31, which called for a monoplane aircraft capable of carrying bombs or 24 troops.

Bren - The Bren Gun, was a series of light machine gun introduced in 1938 and remaining in production until 1971, it was used in a variety of roles until 1991. While best known for its role as the British and Commonwealth forces' primary infantry light machine gun (LMG) in World War II, it was also used in the Korean War and saw service throughout the latter half of the 20th century, including the 1982 Falklands War and the 1991. It could also be mounted on a tripod or vehicle-mounted.

Dingo - The Dingo Scout Car was a light armoured car built in Australia during the Second World War. They were produced by the Ford motor company during 1942. Powered by a Ford V8 with 85 or 95hp, it weighed 4.5 tons and was armed with a Bren Light machine gun.

Douglas DC3 – The DC3 was a twin-engine passenger and transport aircraft that first flew 17 December 1935. Powered initially by two Wright R-1820 Cyclone 9-cyl air-cooled radial piston engines developing 1,100 HP. Its lasting impact on the airline industry and World War II makes it one of the most significant transport aircraft ever made. The major military version was designated the C-47 Skytrain, of which more than 10,000 were produced.

Fi-156 - The Fieseler Fi 156 Storch (English: Stork) was a small German liaison aircraft built by Fieseler before and during World War II. Its first flight was in May 1936. Production continued in other countries into the 1950s for the private market. It remains famous to this day for its excellent STOL performance.

Gloster Gladiator - The Gladiator was a biplane fighter built by the British Gloster Aircraft Company. It was used by the RAF and the FAA (Fleet Air Arm) as the Sea Gladiator variant. It was exported to a number of other air forces during the late 1930s. It was the RAF's last biplane fighter aircraft and was rendered obsolete by newer monoplane designs even as it was being introduced. Though often pitted against more formidable aircraft during the early days of the Second World War, it acquitted itself reasonably well in combat.

Jeep - The Willys MB U.S. Army Jeep (formally the Truck, 1/4 ton, 4x4) and the Ford GPW were manufactured from 1941 to 1945. These small four-wheel drive utility vehicles are considered the iconic World War II Jeep and inspired many similar light utility vehicles such as the original Land Rover. With a simple three-speed gearbox coupled to a Willys L134 2.2L engine producing 60hp and lightweight construction the Jeep weighed just 1040kg.

Junkers Ju 87 – The Ju 87 or Stuka (from Sturzkampfflugzeug, "dive bomber") was a two-man (pilot and rear gunner) single engine, fixed undercarriage and inverted gull wings. It was designed as a very accurate dive-bomber and ground-attack aircraft. Designed by Hermann Pohlmann, the Stuka first flew in 1935 and made its combat debut in 1936 as part of the Luftwaffe's Condor Legion during the Spanish Civil War. The Stuka's design included several new at the time features, including automatic pull-up dive brakes under both wings to ensure that the aircraft recovered from its attack dive even if the pilot blacked out from the high acceleration. The Ju 87 was an easy target for modern fighters of the time and suffered heavy losses during the Battle of Britain due to its poor manoeuvrability and speed.

Junkers Ju-52 - The Ju 52 was a German trimotor transport aircraft manufactured from 1932 to 1945. It saw both civilian and military service during the 1930s and 1940s. Its first flight was in October 1930 and continued in service with civilian airlines until 1952.

Messerschmitt Bf 109 – The Bf 109 was a single engine German fighter aircraft designed by Willy Messerschmitt and Robert Lusser during the early to mid-1930s. It was one of the first truly modern fighters of the era, including such features as all-metal monocoque construction, a closed canopy, a retractable landing gear, and was powered by a liquid-cooled, inverted-V12 aero engine. It first flew in May 1935 and was powered by a Daimler-Benz DB 605A-1 liquid-cooled inverted V12, developing 1,455 HP. It was still being used by the Spanish Air Force up to 1965. The Bf 109 has the accolade in scoring more aerial kills than any other aircraft during World War 2.

Messerschmitt Bf 110 - The Bf 110 was a twin-engine heavy fighter (Zerstörer—German for "Destroyer") in the service of the Luftwaffe during World War II. Hermann Göring was a proponent of the Bf 110, and nicknamed it his Eisenseiten ("Ironsides"). It made its first flight in 1936 and was introduced to the Luftwaffe in 1937. The Bf 110 soldiered on until the end of the war in various roles.

Messerschmitt Me 262 - The Me 262 was world's first operational jet-powered fighter aircraft. Powered by two Junkers Jumo 004 turbojet engines. Design work started before World War II began, however engine problems prevented the aircraft from attaining operational status with the Luftwaffe until mid-1944. Compared with Allied fighters of its day, including the British jet-powered Gloster Meteor, it was much faster and better armed. It was one of the most advanced aviation designs in operational use during World War II, and the helped the Americans after the war develop aircraft such as the F86 Sabre. The Me 262 was used in a variety of roles, including light bomber, reconnaissance and even experimental night fighter versions.

Mortar – A Mortar is a weapons system that consists of an adjustable tube that points upwards usually mounted on a tripod type design. Rocket propelled grenades are then dropped into the tube to be fired at a set target. They come in a variety of sizes and are highly effective against soft targets. Larger mortars can have some success against more hardened target. The rounds can be either HE (High Explosive) or Smoke.

P47 Thunderbolt – The P47 was a single engine fighter bomber powered by a Pratt & Whitney R-2800 Double Wasp engine. It was the heaviest fighter of World War Two and used in a variety of roles, from bomber escort to bombing and interdiction. It had its first flight in May 1941 and 15,560 went on to be built by the end of the War. Due to its air-cooled engine, it had a much greater survivability than many other contemporary fighters of the day.

Panzerfaust - The Panzerfaust ("Tank fist", or Pzf in short.) These simple but effective anti-tank weapons proved to be devastating against Allied tanks during second half of the war, and, more important, these weapons set the pattern for most post-war developments in the field of man-portable antitank weapons. The Panzerfaust 60M doubled the effective range of fire from 30 to 60 meters by using launching tube / barrel of larger calibre and more powerful propellant charge. The actual warhead stayed the same. In November 1944 a further improved version appeared, the Panzerfaust 100M, which extended effective range to 100 meters by using a tandem propellant charge. The semi-experimental Panzerfaust 150M served as a pattern for first Soviet post-war RPG, the RPG-2

PIAT - The PIAT (Projector, Infantry, Anti-Tank) was a British handheld anti-tank weapon developed during the Second World War. The PIAT was designed in 1942 in response to the British Army's need for a more effective infantry anti-tank weapon, and entered service in 1943. The PIAT was based on the spigot mortar system, which launched a 1.1 kg bomb using a powerful spring and a cartridge on the tail of the projectile. It possessed an effective range of approximately 110 m in a direct fire anti-tank role, and 320 m in an indirect fire 'house-breaking' role. The PIAT had several advantages over other infantry anti-tank weapons of the period, which included a lack of muzzle smoke to reveal the position of the user, and an inexpensive barrel; however, this was countered by, amongst other things, a difficulty in cocking the weapon, the bruising the user received when firing it, and problems with its penetrative power.

Sherman Tank - The Sherman evolved from the Grant and Lee medium tanks. It kept quite a bit of the previous mechanical design, but added a main 75 mm gun mounted on a fully traversing turret, with a gyrostabiliser enabling the crew to fire with reasonable accuracy while the tank was on the move. The designers ensured it had mechanical reliability, ease of production and maintenance, durability, standardisation of parts. Although being a petrol engine with a 400hp and later 470hp they were prone to catching fire. These factors made the Sherman superior in some regards to the earlier German light and medium tanks of 1939-41. The Sherman ended up being produced in large numbers and formed the backbone of most of the Allied offensives, starting in late 1942.

Short Stirling – The Stirling was the first four-engined British heavy bomber of the Second World War. Powered by four Bristol Hercules II radial engine, producing 1,375 HP. The Stirling was designed and built by Short Brothers to an Air Ministry specification from 1936. It had its first flight on 14 May 1939 and entered service in 1941. The Stirling had a relatively brief operational career as a bomber, being relegated to second line duties as more of a transport plane from 1943 onwards when other four-engined RAF bombers such as the Lancaster and Halifax, took over its role, but fulfilled a major role as a glider tug and resupply aircraft during the allied invasion of France.

SS – These were the defence corps of the Nazi party and commanded by Himmler. The SS was a major paramilitary organisation under Adolf Hitler and the Nazi Party. It began at the end of 1920 as a small, permanent guard unit known as the "Saal-Schutz" (Hall-Protection) made up of NSDAP volunteers to provide security for Nazi Party meetings in Munich. Later in 1925, Heinrich Himmler joined the unit, which had by then been reformed and renamed the "Schutz-Staffel". Under Himmler's leadership (1929–45), it grew from a small paramilitary formation to one of the largest and most powerful organizations in Nazi Germany. Built upon the Nazi ideology, the SS under Himmler's command was responsible for many of the crimes against humanity during World War II.

Very Pistol – The Very pistol was used in the Second World War to fire flares and are of a one inch bore (26.5mm). These are still available and more recent longer barrel models can also fire parachute flares.

Vickers Machine Gun - The Vickers machine gun or Vickers gun is a name primarily used to refer to the water-cooled .303 British (7.7 mm) machine gun produced by Vickers Limited, originally for the British Army. It served from before the First World War until the 1960s, with air-cooled versions of it serving on World

War I aircraft of many of the Allied air forces' fighters a few of which served during the Second World War. Later adopted by the SAS and mounted onto their Jeeps.

Known Members of the SAS in World War II

(Des) Peter Middleton (1SAS)
Albert Youngman (1SAS)
Alex Griffiths (1SAS)
Alex Robertson (2SAS)
Alf Dignum (1SAS)
Andree Lemee (4SAS French)
Arthur Huntbach (2SAS)
Arthur Thomson (1SAS)
Augustin Jordan (4SAS French)
Bill Deakins (1SAS)
Bill Fraser (1SAS)
Bill Robinson (2SAS)
Bill Stirling (2SAS) Commanding Officer 2SAS and brother of David Stirling
Billy Stalker (1SAS)
Bob Francis (1SAS)
Bob Lowson (1SAS)
Bob McDougall - (1SAS)
Bob Walker-Brown (2SAS)
Charlie Hackney (2SAS)
Cyril Radford (2SAS)
Cyril Wheeler (2SAS)
David Danger (1SAS)
Dennis Wainman (1SAS)
Doug Cronk (1SAS)
Duncan Ridler (1SAS)
Ernest Thomas "Bob" Lilley (1SAS) Regimental Sergeant Major. 'L' Detachment, awarded MM, BEM, MID.
Frank Hughes (2SAS) DCM
Freddie Oakes (2SAS)
George Daniels (2SAS)
George Danies (1SAS)
Granville Burne (2SAS)
Guy Le Citol (4SAS French)

Harry Poat (1SAS)
Harry Vickers (2SAS)
Harry Wilkins (1SAS)
Henry Druce (2SAS)
Jack Paley (2SAS)
Jacques Goffinet (Belgian SAS)
James McDiarmid (1SAS)
Jean Czarski (4SAS French)
Jean Switters (Belgian SAS)
Jean-Claude Heilporn (Belgian SAS)
Jeff Du Vivier (1SAS)
Jim "Gentleman Jim" Almonds (1SAS) 'L Detachment'
Jimmy Storie (1SAS)
Jock Lewes - Co-founder of the SAS
Joe Paley (2SAS)
Joe Patterson (2SAS)
John Noble (1SAS)
John Randall (1SAS)
John William Bickers (1SAS)
Johnny Cooper (1SAS)
Ken Harvey (2SAS)
Malcolm Pleydell (1SAS)
Marc Mora (3SAS French)
Marc Mouflin (4SAS French)
Maurice Duno (3SAS French)
Mike Alexandre (4SAS French)
Mike Sadler (1SAS)
Nathaniel Kennedy (1SAS)
Neil McMillan (1SAS)
Paddy Mayne, DSO – (1SAS) One of the original SAS Officers with 'L' Detachment
Peter Davis (1SAS)
Peter Weaver (1SAS)
Philip Schlee (1SAS)
Ray Rogers (2SAS)
Reg 'Nobby' Redington (1SAS) DCM
Reg Seekings (1SAS)

Renee Roberts (2SAS)
Richard Bond (1SAS)
Robert McDougall (1SAS)
Robert Piron (Belgian SAS)
Roger Boutinot (4SAS French)
Ronald Grierson (1SAS)
Ross Littlejohn (2SAS)
Roy Close (1SAS)
Roy Farran (2SAS)
Sid Payne (1SAS)
Sir David Stirling OBE DSO - Founder of the SAS
Tommy Langton (1SAS)
Tony Greville-Bell (2SAS)
Tony Marsh (1SAS)
Vic Long (1SAS)
Yvan Brasseur (Belgian SAS)

Main SAS Operations during World War II

Crusader Initial unsuccessful raid by 'L' Detachment to secure Airfields in Libya.

Squatter 16/17 November 1941 raid on forward Axis airfields in North Africa.

Bigamy September 1942, raid on the Port of Benghazi.

Chestnut 12 July 1943 raids supporting Sicily invasion to disrupt communications, transport and the enemy in general.

Narcissus 10 July 1943, capture of lighthouse in Sicily.

Begonia/Jonquil 2 October 1943, rescue of POWs in Italy.

Candytuft October 1943 raid on railroad targets in Italy.

Baobab January 1944, raid on rail targets serving Anzio, Italy.

Titanic June 6, 1944, along with the RAF, the objective of the operation was to drop 500 dummy parachutists in places other than the actual drop zones to be used, to confuse the Germans.

Nelson June 1944, planned operation in the Orleans Gap that never happened.

Samwest 6 June 1944, 4SAS dropped in Côtes-du-Nord Brittany their objective was to hinder movement of German troops.

Grog 5 June, 1944 4SAS in conjunction with Operations Dingson and Samwest, their objective was to hinder movement of German troops.

Dingson 6 June 1944, 4SAS Battalion dropped into Morbihan, Brittany to hinder movement of German troops.

Bulbasket 6 June 1944, 2SAS failed operation to block the Paris to Bordeaux railway line near Poitiers and to hamper German reinforcements heading towards the Normandy beachheads.

Cooney 8 June 1944, 18 teams of the 4SAS Battalion dropped into Brittany to break communications lines.

Houndsworth 6 June 1944, their objective was to disrupt German lines of communication, coordinate the activities of the French Resistance and prevent German reinforcements moving to the Normandy beachheads.

Lost 23 June 1944, British and French SAS operation in Brittany.

Defoe 19 July 1944, SAS patrols in Normandy.

Gaff 18 July 1944, attempt to kill or capture Erwin Rommel.

Dunhill 3 August 1944, raid in support of the breakout from the Normandy beachhead.

Loyton 12 August 1944, operations near the Belfort Gap.

Newton 19 August 1944, attacks on German rear areas.

Noah August 1944, attack on retreating Germans in Belgium.

Canuck January 1945, operation in Northern Italy.

Cold Comfort 17 February 1945, failed SAS raid on railroad targets near Verona.

Tombola 4 March 1945, major operation around Bologna.

Archway March 1945, reconnaissance in support of the crossing of the Rhine. One of the largest operations undertaken by the SAS during the Second World War.

Amherst 7 April 1945 Over 600 French 3 and 4SAS were dropped into Holland between Hoogeveen and Groningen to support advancing allied forces.

Keystone 7April 1945, operation near Ijsselmeer a patrol consisting of a number of jeeps to attack German positions and vehicles.

Howard 9 April 1945 was a reconnaissance mission acting as reconnaissance for the 4th Canadian Armoured Division.

Appendix I

World War 2 was a global war, which lasted from 1939 to 1945. It involved nearly all of the world's nations, including the major world powers. The war led to the formation of two opposing military alliances - the Allies and the Axis. It became the most widespread war in history, with more than 100 million people serving in military units from over 30 different countries. In a state of "total war", the major participants placed their entire economic, industrial, and scientific capabilities at the service of the war effort, with everything produced pretty much going into the war effort. Marked by mass deaths of civilians, including the Holocaust and the only use of nuclear weapons in warfare, it resulted in between 50 million to maybe over 75 million fatalities. The number of fatalities makes World War II the biggest loss of life due to war so far in human history.

World War 2 is thought to have begun on 1 September 1939 with the invasion of Poland by Germany and subsequent declarations of war on Germany by France and Britain. From late 1939 to early 1941, in a series of campaigns and treaties, Germany formed the Axis alliance with Italy, conquering or subduing much of continental Europe. The speed of the initial German advance was remarkable and labelled 'Blitzkrieg'. The North African campaign was the turning point for the Allies with the defeat of Rommel in North Africa. The war in Europe ended with an invasion of Germany by the Western Allies and the Soviet Union culminating in the capture of Berlin and dividing Germany into West Germany and East Germany under communist rule until the fall of the Berlin wall in 1989 and the breakup of the USSR. The German unconditional surrender came on 8 May 1945. Following the Potsdam Declaration by the Allies on 26 July 1945, the United States dropped atomic bombs on the Japanese cities of Hiroshima on 6 August, and Nagasaki on 9 August. With an invasion of the Japanese archipelago imminent, and the Soviet Union having declared war on Japan by invading Manchuria, Japan surrendered on 15 August 1945, ending the war in Asia giving a total victory to the Allies over the Axis.

World War 2 altered the political and social landscape of the world. The UN (United Nations) was established to help support international cooperation and prevent future conflicts. The Soviet Union and the United States emerged as rival superpowers after World War II, setting the stage for the Cold War, which lasted for the next 46 years. Meanwhile, the influence of European great powers started to decline, while the decolonisation of Asia and Africa began. Most countries whose industries had been damaged moved towards economic recovery. Political integration, especially in Europe, emerged as an effort to stabilise post-war relations and fight more effectively in the Cold War.

World War 2 Timeline

1938 - German Anschluss with Austria, Hitler went ahead with his plans to unify all German-speaking people. He annexed Austria then demanded the liberation of German people in the Sudetenland region of Czechoslovakia. Neville Chamberlain flew to Germany to attempt a settlement before war broke out.

30 Sept 1938 - Treaty of Munich, Hitler, Chamberlain, Daladier of France and Mussolini of Italy met in Munich and agreed that Hitler should have the Sudetenland of Czechoslovakia. The Czechs were not represented at the meeting and realising that no country would come to their aid was forced to surrender the Sudetenland to Germany. Hitler assured those at the meeting that this was the extent of his ambitions for expansion. Chamberlain returned to England with a piece of paper signed by Hitler, proclaiming 'peace in our time.'

March 1939 - Hitler invades Czechoslovakia, Despite the assurances given by Hitler in the Treaty of Munich (Sept 1938), he marched into Czechoslovakia and occupied the country.

March - April 1939 - Britain rearms and reassures Poland Britain had begun re-arming and a highly secret radar early warning system was installed along the east coast. Conscription was introduced and assurances were given to Poland, who was being threatened by the Fuhrer.

Late Aug 1939 - Russia and Germany sign pact, Hitler and Stalin signed a non-aggression pact, which included secret clauses for the division of Poland.

1 Sept 1939 - Hitler invades Poland

3 Sept 1939 - Britain and France declared war on Germany. Neville Chamberlain broadcast the announcement that the country was at war.

Sept 1939-May 1940 - 'Phoney War' the months following Britain's declaration of war are referred to as the 'phoney war' because Britain saw no military action.

April-May 1940 - Hitler invades Denmark and Norway Hitler invaded and occupied Denmark and Norway to safeguard supply routes of Swedish ore and also to establish a Norwegian base from which to break the British naval blockade on Germany.

10 May 1940 Blitzkrieg - Hitler launched his blitzkrieg (lightning war) against Holland and Belgium. Rotterdam was bombed almost to extinction. Both countries were occupied.

13 May 1940 - Neville Chamberlain resigned after pressure from Labour members for a more active prosecution of the war and Winston Churchill became the new head of the wartime coalition government. Chamberlain gave Churchill his unreserved support. Ernest Bevin was made minister of labour and recruited workers for the factories and stepped up coal production. Lord Beaverbrook, minister of Aircraft Production increased production of fighter aircraft.

26 May 1940 - Operation Dynamo, the British commander-in-chief, General Gort, had been forced to retreat to the coast at Dunkirk. The troops waited, under merciless fire, to be taken off the beaches. A call went out to all owners of seaworthy vessels to travel to Dunkirk to take the troops off the beaches of Dunkirk. More than 338,000 men were rescued, among them some 140,000 French who would form the nucleus of the Free French army under a little known general, Charles de Gaulle.

11 June 1940 - Italy entered the war on the side of the Axis powers. Italy's motive for entering the war was the hope of rich pickings from the spoils of war.

22 June 1940 - The French, Marshall Petain, signed an armistice with Germany taking France, which had been devastated, out of the war and into German occupation.

10 July - 31 October 1940 - Battle of Brittan, the Battle of Britain comprised four phases:

1. During July Hitler sent his Luftwaffe bombers to attack British ports. His aim was also to assess the speed and quality of response by the RAF.

2. During August the attacks on shipping continued but bombing raids were concentrated on RAF airfields.

3. The Blitz - From September 7th the city of London was heavily bombed. Hitler hoped to destroy the morale of the British people.

4. Night Bombing - With the failure of daylight bombing raids Hitler began a series of nightly bombing raids on London and other important industrial cities.

The RAF defended the skies and by October 31 the raids had ceased.

22 Sept 1940 - Tripartite Pact, this pact of mutual alliance was signed by Germany, Italy and Japan.

December 1940 - British rout Italians in N. Africa Italian forces in North Africa were routed by the British led by General Wavell.

Early 1941 - German and Italian troops attacked Yugoslavia, Greece and the island of Crete. German field Marshall Erwin Rommel led the axis powers back to North Africa.

22 June 1941 - Hitler attacks Russia - Operation Barbarossa, Hitler sends 3 million soldiers and 3,500 tanks into Russia. The Russians were taken by surprise as they had signed a treaty with Germany in 1939. Stalin immediately signed a mutual assistance treaty with Britain and launched an Eastern front battle that would claim 20 million casualties. The USA, which had been supplying arms to Britain under a 'Lend-Lease' agreement, offered similar aid to USSR.

7 Dec 1941 - Pearl Harbour, the Japanese, who were already waging war against the Chinese, attacked the US pacific fleet at Pearl Harbour, Hawaii, as a preliminary to taking British, French and Dutch colonies in South East Asia.

8 Dec 1941 - Britain and America declare war on Japan

Feb 1942 - The Japanese captured Singapore from the British, taking some 60,000 prisoners.

June 1942 - Battle of Midway, America defeated the Japanese navy at the Battle of Midway. Following this victory, the US Navy was able to push the Japanese back.

Aug 1942 - Allies in N. Africa. General Alexander was given a hand-written directive from Churchill ordering that his main directive was to be the destruction of the German-Italian army commanded by Field-Marshall Rommel together with all its supplies and establishments in Egypt and Libya. As soon as sufficient material had been built up, Alexander handed the campaign over to General Montgomery.

23 Oct 1942 - Battle of El Alamein, Montgomery attacked the German-Italian army in North Africa with a massive bombardment followed by an armoured attack. He then proceeded to chase the routed enemy some 1500 miles across the desert.

Nov 1942 - Battle of Stalingrad, the Russians won their first victory against Germany at the Battle of Stalingrad.

Nov 1942 - Allies push into N. Africa; the British and American forces under the command of General Dwight Eisenhower landed in the NW of Africa and assumed control of French Morocco and Algeria. They gradually closed in on the Germans.

May 12 1943 - Axis surrenders when the British and American forces managed to defeat the Axis forces in North Africa.

July 1943 Allies invade Sicily

Aug 1943 - Allies take Sicily

3 Sept 1943 - Italy surrenders, Mussolini had been thrown out of office and the new government of Italy surrendered to the British and the USA. They then agreed to join the allies. The Germans took control of the Italian army, freed Mussolini from imprisonment and set him up as head of a puppet government in

Northern Italy. This blocked any further allied advance through Italy.

Nov 1943 - Allies meet at Tehran, Stalin, Roosevelt and Churchill met to co-ordinate plans for a simultaneous squeeze on Germany. They also discussed post war settlements. Churchill mistrusted Stalin; Roosevelt anxious to show that the West would not stand against Russia, went along with Stalin's wishes for a second front in France and no diversions further east. Churchill was over-ruled and the fate of post-war Eastern Europe was thus decided.

Jan 1944 - Leningrad relieved after the siege of Leningrad was lifted by the Soviet army.

June 1944 - Rome liberated, although Italy had surrendered in September, it was only now that the allies were able to liberate Rome from the Germans.

6 June 1944 - D-Day, the allies launched an attack on Germany's forces in Normandy, Western France. Thousands of transports carried an invasion army under the supreme command of General Eisenhower to the Normandy beaches. The Germans who had been fed false information about a landing near Calais, rushed troops to the area but were unable to prevent the allies from forming a solid bridgehead. For the allies it was essential to first capture a port.

July 1944 - Japanese evicted from Burma, British forces under General Slim, with help from guerrilla-fighting Chindits led by Orde Wingate, evicted the Japanese from Burma.

25 Aug 1944 - Paris liberated, the French capital of Paris was liberated from the Germans.

8 Sept 1944 - First V2 Flying bombs start attacking London.

Dec 1944 - Battle of the Bulge, Germany launched its final defensive through the Ardennes region of Belgium. However, they were beaten back by the allies.

March 1945 - Allies cross the Rhine; the Allies crossed the Rhine while Soviet forces were approaching Berlin from the East.

12 April 1945 - President Roosevelt died. He was succeeded by President Truman.

April 1945 - Russians reach Berlin shortly before the American forces.

28 April 1945 - Mussolini captured and executed after partisans captured Mussolini and executed him.

30 April 1945 - Adolf Hitler commits suicide in his bombproof shelter together with his mistress, Eva Braun, who he had, at the last minute, made his wife.

2 May 1945 - German forces in Italy surrendered to the Allies.

4 May 1945 - German forces in North West Germany, Holland and Denmark surrendered to Montgomery on Luneburg Heath. Admiral Donitz, whom Hitler had nominated as his successor, tried to reach agreement to surrender to the Western allies but to continue to fight the Russians. His request was refused.

7 May 1945 - Hitler's successor, Admiral Donitz, offered an unconditional surrender to the allies.

8 May 1945 - V.E. day (celebrated 7 May in Commonwealth countries)

5 July 1945 - Winston Churchill lost the election to Clement Atlee's Labour Party. The Labour party promised sweeping social reforms including nationalisation of the coal and railway industries and the creation of a welfare state. The Labour party gained 393 seats to the Conservatives 213. It was generally accepted that the landslide victory for Labour was due to the men and women of the armed services who did not want to resume civilian life under the conditions that they had before they entered service.

6 Aug 1945 – First Atomic bomb dropped on the Japanese city of Hiroshima by the Americans and the Japanese generals refused to surrender.

8 Aug 1945 - Russia declared war on Japan and invaded Japanese-ruled Manchuria.

9 Aug 1945 - America drops a second atomic bomb on the port of Nagasaki as the Japanese had not surrendered following Hiroshima.

14 Aug 1945 - The Japanese unconditionally surrendered to the allies ending the Second World War.

2 Sept 1945 - American General, Douglas MacArthur, accepted Japan's surrender thus formally ending the Second World War.

APPENDIX II

SAS after World War II

1947 - May 1st - the SAS is revived in the form of 21st Battalion, Army Air Corps SAS a Territorial Army Unit.

1950 - 21 SAS deploy to the Korean War.

1950 - 1955 Malaya - 21 SAS deploy to Malaya, renamed as the 'Malayan Scouts', in response to the 'Malayan Emergency' insurrection. Much of the Regiment's expertise in jungle warfare are learnt in this period.

1952 -The SAS is reorganised into 22nd Special Air Service Regiment and 21st Special Air Service Regiment.

1958 - 1959 Oman - The SAS was deployed to the Gulf state of Oman, battling forces opposed to the Sultan.

1959 - The 23rd Special Air Service Regiment, a Territorial Army (reserve forces) unit, is created.

1963 - 1966 - Counter Insurgency, the SAS support guerrillas during the Indonesia-Malaysia confrontation in Borneo, Brunei and Sarawak

1964 - 1967 – Aden, the SAS deploy for counter-insurgency operations in the British protectorate.

1970 - 1977 - Dhofor, Oman, the SAS are sent to Oman to fight against another insurrection.

1972 - Counter Terrorism, following the intervention by German police during the Munich hostage crisis that went wrong, the SAS create the Counter-Revolutionary War wing. The CRW wing begins developing techniques for both counter-terrorism and body-guarding operations.

1972 - The QE2, when a bomb-threat is issued against the QE2, a team comprising of SAS/SBS & Army bomb disposal experts parachute into the sea, board the liner and perform a search. No bomb was found.

1975 - Stansted hijacking when the SAS's first real test of their techniques developed by the CRW wing, the SAS storm a hijacked airliner at Stansted airport. Using non-lethal force, they arrest the lone hijacker.

1975 - The Balcombe Street Siege, was when an IRA operation ends with a family being held hostage in a London flat. As the SAS prepare to intervene, news of their arrival is leaked to the media. Upon hearing this news, the IRA men promptly surrender to police. Without a bullet being fired.

1976 - The SAS deploy to Northern Ireland. In response to the worsening crisis in Northern Ireland, the SAS, who had been over the water in small numbers since 1973, mostly in advisory roles, are now deployed directly in strength to take on the IRA, following targets, gathering intelligence and take downs.

1977 - Lufthansa hijacking, when a German Airliner is hijacked by terrorists, GSG-9, the German counter-terrorist unit, receives assistance from the SAS. Two SAS soldiers accompany the GSG-9 assault team as they pursue the hijacked airliner to Mogadishu, Somalia. As the GSG-9 team stormed the cabin, the two SAS men threw stun grenades to distract the hijackers.

1980 - Operation Nimrod, B Squadron, storm the Iranian Embassy in London after twenty six hostages are taken.

1981 - The Gambia, in August 1981, three SAS men were sent to the Gambia to assist President Jawara's regime in putting down a coup attempt by Cuban-backed Marxist rebels. Hostages taken by the rebels included members of the President's family. The three man SAS team managed to rescue all of the hostages and help restore Jawara to power.

1982 - The Falklands the SAS play a major part in the British campaign to retake the Falkland Islands from Argentine invaders. This included gathering intelligence, acting as target spotters for the Harrier and going back to their World War Two roots blowing up aircraft on Pebble Island.

1982 -1989 – Afghanistan, following the invasion of Afghanistan by the Soviet Union in 1979, a number of SAS men were sent to advise anti-Soviet forces in Afghanistan. These men officially 'leave' the Regiment to be hired by a front company of the SIS, Britain's secret service. They are then contracted to go to Afghanistan where they link up with Afghani rebels. The SAS men lead the rebels on hit-and-run missions against Russian supply convoys. Once US-made Stinger SAMs become available, the SAS instruct the Mujahidin on their use. Some Afghanis are brought over to the UK and trained by SAS instructors.

1984 - Libyan Embassy in London In April 1984, the SAS anti-terrorist team deployed to London and stormed the Libyan embassy following the shooting of British policewoman from a shot fired within the embassy. A diplomatic solution was reached and the SAS were stood down.

1985 – Botswana, following a series of cross-border attacks by South African forces, B Squadron provide training to the Botswana Defence Force (BDF).

1987 - Peterhead Prison, in a quite controversial use of the SAS in a domestic situation, a team of SAS are sent to quell the riots at Peterhead Prison and rescue a Prison Warder being held hostage. The SAS used Batons, stun grenades and CS gas, rather than lethal force and their quick attack meant the hostage was rescued without injury to the SAS, hostage or prisoners.

1988-1989 – Beirut, the SAS deploy to Beirut to prepare the ground for a rescue of kidnapped Western hostages including Terry Waite and John McCarthy. Covert teams carry out surveillance of possible insertion/extraction sites and routes in/out but in the end the mission is called off.

1988 – Gibraltar, three suspected IRA terrorists are shot dead by the SAS on the streets of Gibraltar in the controversial 'Operation Flavius'.

1989 - 1991 – Columbia SAS teams train and assist Columbian forces in their struggle against the drug, cartels.

1991 - Gulf War A, D & part of B Squadron deploy to the Gulf in response to Saddam Hussein's invasion of Kuwait. As Iraq invades Kuwait, A British Airways passenger plane, Flight 149, stops at Kuwait International Airport in order to deliver a group of men, speculated to be SAS operatives. The action causes the plane's passengers to be detained by the Iraqis and form part of Saddam's 'human shield'. A & D squadron Land Rover columns drive far behind Iraqi lines initially on search and destroy operations, then later becoming part of efforts to find and destroy Iraqi Scud missile launchers. B Squadron insert foot patrols to watch main supply routes (MSRs) for Scud convoys.

One patrol, Bravo Two Zero, are compromised and try to escape and evade to Syria.

1991 – Zaire, a small SAS team is sent to protect the British Embassy in the troubled African nation of Zaire. Whilst there, the SAS ensure that all British diplomatic staff are safely evacuated from the country.

1993 - The Waco Siege, One or two SAS soldiers are sent to advise US authorities over the siege of the Branch Davidian cult at Waco, Texas.

1994/95 - Bosnia, the SAS support the UN peacekeeping efforts in Bosnia and become caught up in the siege of Gorazde.

1995 - Sierra Leone, a two man SAS team are sent to Sierra Leone to carry out intelligence gathering and a feasibility study for a possible rescue of westerners taken hostage by African rebels. All hostages are eventually released without need for any military intervention.

1997 - Lima, Peru, the SAS advises the Peruvian authorities on a commando raid to end a four-month siege of the Japanese embassy in Lima. One of the hostages dies in the operation, together with two Peruvian commandos and 14 hostage-takers.

1997 – Bosnia SAS teams, working under a NATO remit, arrest several suspected war criminals.

1997 – Albania, in late March, the SAS extract British Aid Worker, Robert Welch from war-torn Albania. The 4-man SAS team, in a two Land Rover convoy meet Welch at a prearranged point then drive him to a helicopter landing zone. Two Chinooks land and a security force made up of troops from The Prince of Wales Royal Regiment debussed and fanned out around the landing zone. The two SAS Land Rovers, including Welch, are driven up into the Chinook's cargo hold and shortly after the rescue force is airborne, flying low across the Albanian countryside and out to sea for a refuelling stop on an American Aircraft Carrier stationed in the Adriatic.

A day later, a British couple, Mike and Judy Smith, were safely escorted to safety by the SAS. The Smiths were running an orphanage in Elbasan, in the Albania countryside and had phoned the British embassy in the capital, Tirana, when a series of gang-related killings cause them to fear for the children in their care. An SAS convoy of 3 vehicles drive to the orphanage and set up secure satellite communications. The British couple are given 30 minutes to prepare themselves and the 22 children to move. As the convoy drives towards the relative safety of Tirana, 2 RAF Chinooks escort them, ready to land and evacuate the passengers if needed. The SAS, with the British couple and children arrive in Tirana without incident.

1998 - The Gulf, a Small numbers of SAS and SBS forces are deployed to the Persian Gulf to act as Combat Search and Rescue (CSAR) forces for downed allied air crew during the US-led bombing of Iraqi targets in the second Gulf war.

1999 – Kosovo, the SAS play a part in the NATO intervention against the Serbian action in Kosovo

2000 - An Afghani Boeing 727 airliner is hijacked and flown to Stansted Airport in February 2000. The SAS anti-terrorist team deploys and prepares to storm the plane if necessary. The drama comes to a peaceful end as it emerges that the hijack was an immigration ploy by some of the passengers.

2000 - Sierra Leone Summer 2000: SAS patrols carry out fact-finding missions in support of the UN mission in the war-torn African nation.

May 23 - A small SAS team secure RUF leader Foday Sankoh during violent clashes in the Capital, Freetown. Sankoh is spirited away to British custody.

June 15 - SAS spotters on the ground help to guide Indian and British helicopters in rescuing more than 200 UN observers and soldiers held hostage by Revolutionary United Front rebels. (Operation Khukri)

September 2000: When British Soldiers are held hostage by rebels, the SAS lead a daring rescue mission to free them. The was a joint mission with the PARA's

2001 – Macedonia, the SAS deploy to Macedonia as part of efforts to prevent another large-scale Balkans conflict.

2001 – Afghanistan, in the aftermath of the terrorist attacks of September 11th, the SAS deploy to Afghanistan and undertake reconnaissance missions along with operations to capture key

Taliban figures. The SAS also carried out a large-scale assault on an opium processing plant doubling as a Taliban/Al-Qaeda base in 'Operation Trent'.

2003 to date – Iraq The SAS played a role in the US-led invasion of Iraq although the precise details of their involvement are not publicly known as yet. They supported America Delta Force and SEAL teams in a variety of missions. Following the initial invasion, the SAS work with TF-121 (now TF-88), a US-led team of Special Operations units tasked with hunting down high-value members of Saddam's regime as well as targeting Al-Qaeda. The SAS commit a full Squadron to 'Task Force Black'.

2004 - October - The SAS is put on standby to rescue kidnapped British citizen, Ken Bigley who is later killed by his captors.

2005 - July - A 16-man SAS sniper team kill three suicide bombers as they leave their house in Baghdad.

2005 - 19th September - The SAS rescue 2 SRR operatives who had been held by Iraqi police with alleged links to the insurgency.

2006 - 23rd March - Members of B Squadron, SAS, rescue British peace activist, Norman Kmber + 2 Canadians from their kidnappers in Baghdad.

2004 - Testing Security at GCHQ, A joint SAS/SBS team infiltrate GCHQ, Britain's communications intelligence headquarters as a part of a security exercise.

2005 - The Olympics, the SAS, along with the SBS, are sent to Greece to advise the Greek authorities and to protect visiting British dignitaries against the threat of terrorism.

2005 - July bombings, following 2 waves of terrorist attacks in London, UK Special Forces, including the SAS, SBS and SRR deploy on the streets of British cities, assessing security weak points and providing rapid-response support to police operations. SAS troopers, skilled in explosive entry, assist the Met Armed Response unit, C019, in arresting suspected terrorists.

2007 – Somalia, the SAS reportedly deploy to Somalia in January, tracking down Al-Qaeda members fleeing from US air strikes.

2007 – London 22 January - An SAS unit is reportedly permanently deployed to London in order to assist the Police in counter terrorist operations

2007 – Ethiopia March 7 - The SAS is put on standby to intervene in the kidnapping of Britons in Ethiopia.

2007 – Baghdad, September - The SAS joins the hunt for an Al-Qaeda killer operating in Baghdad.

2011 – SAS and MI6 operatives were captured by the Libyan rebels and had their weapons taken, they were later released.

2012 – Afghanistan, the SAS, along with U.S SEALs launch a rescue mission of four hostages, including a British citizen, Helen Johnston. Five Taliban fighters were killed during the rescue mission.

Bibliography

Alan Hoe, *David Stirling* (Warner books 1992)

Alastair Timpson, Andrew Gibson-Watt *In Rommel's Backyard: A Memoir of the Long Range Desert Group* (Pen & Sword Military; Reprint edition 2010)

Andy Mcnab *Seven Troop* (Corgi 2009)

Antony Kemp *The SAS at War 1941-1945* (Murray 1991)

Antony Kemp *The SAS at War: 1941-1945* (Penguin Books Ltd; New edition 2000)

Brian Lett *SAS in Tuscany 1943-45* (Pen & Sword Books Ltd 2011)

David Lloyd-Owen *The Long Range Desert group* (Pen & Sword 1980)

G.B Courtney *SBS in World War Two* (Robert Hale 1983)

Gavin Mortimer *Stirling's Men*: The Inside History of the SAS in World War II (Phoenix; New Ed edition 2005)

Gavin Mortimer *The SAS in World War II*: An Illustrated History (Osprey 2011)

Gordon Stevens *The Originals*: The Secret History of the Birth of the SAS: In Their Own Words (Ebury Press 2006)

Hamish Ross *Paddy Mayne* (The History Press Ltd; New Ed edition 2004)

John Keegan *Six Armies in Normandy* (Pimlico 1992)

John Lewes, Jock Lewes: The Biography of Jock Lewes, Co-founder of the SAS. (Pen & Sword Books Ltd 2001)

John North *North West Europe* (HMSO 1953)

Julian Thompson *The War Behind Enemy Lines* (Macmillan 1999)

Lord carver *The War in Italy* (Pan 2001)

Lorna Almonds *Gentleman Jim* (Robinson 2001)

Marcus Binney *Secret War Heroes*: Men of the Special Operations executive (Hodder & Stoughton 2005)

Martain Dhillon *Rogue Warrior of the SAS*: The Blair Mayne Legend (Mainstream Publishing 2003)

Michael Asher *The Regiment*: The Real Story of the SAS (Penguin 2008)

National Archives *Special Forces in the Desert War* (National Archives 2008)

Philip Vickers *Das Reich, 2nd SS Panzer Division* (Pen & Sword 2000)

Roger Flamand *Amherst* (Atlante 1998)

Sherri Ottis *Silent Heroes* (University of Kentucky 2001)

Tim Moreman Long Range Desert Group Patrolman (Osprey 2010)

William Mackenzie The Secret History of the SOE – Special Operations Executive 1940-1945 (BPR Publications, 2000)

Television

SAS The Originals – History Channel

Articles

Denise Winterman *The SAS secret hidden since World War II* BBC News Magazine 23 September 2011

Printed in Great Britain
by Amazon